YEAR TWO
SPRING

An Inspiring Two-Year Journey Through The Bible

Old Testament Devotional Commentary
NIZAR & ELLEN SHAHEEN

New Testament Devotional Commentary
JIM & KATHY CANTELON

Inspirational "Prayer For Today" portions
DAVID & NORMA-JEAN MAINSE

A ministry of Crossroads Christian Communications Inc.

In Canada:
Crossroads Christian
Communications Inc.
100 Huntley Street
Toronto, Ontario
M4Y 2L1

Bus: (416) 961-8001

In the USA:
Crossroads Christian
Communications Inc.
Box 486
Niagara Falls, NY
14302

Prayer: (416) 961-1500

ISBN 0-921702-16-7
Copyright 1991 ©CROSSROADS CHRISTIAN COMMUNICATIONS INC.

Published by CROSSROADS CHRISTIAN COMMUNICATIONS INC.
100 Huntley Street, Toronto, Ontario, Canada M4Y 2L1

Printed in Canada
Harmony Printing Limited
123 Eastside Drive, Toronto, Ontario, Canada M8Z 5S5

Scripture quotations, unless otherwise marked, are from the New King James Version and are used with permission of Thomas Nelson Publishers. Copyright ©1979, 1980, 1982.

Cover photo by H. Abernathy/Miller Comstock

"The heavens declare the glory of God; And the firmament shows His handiwork. DAY UNTO DAY utters speech, and night unto night reveals knowledge."

— Psalm 19:1,2

Dear Reader,

The phrase, "Day unto day", found in Psalm 19:2, is most meaningful to us all. Our Old Testament devotional commentary writer for this series, Nizar Shaheen, is fluent in the original language of the Old Testament. He tells me that this Hebrew phrase does not just mean "day to day" or "day after day", but rather means "one day flowing into the next without any break." I'm sure this is the way God wants our relationship with Him to be.

Psalm 19:2 is a very special verse to me personally, because God used the words "Day unto day" to speak to me many years ago about the need for daily Christian television and the importance of hearing from God daily through the reading of His Word.

We've entitled this devotional commentary series *Day Unto Day*, after Psalm 19:2. It is designed to guide you through God's Word in two years while giving you fresh devotional thoughts inspired by each day's reading.

This Year Two-Spring volume is the sixth in our eight-volume series. If you have not received the earlier volumes, then you can simply start your two-year journey now and end with the fifth volume in two years time. Please request each volume in writing approximately one month before you'll need it.

My prayer for all who read these volumes is that God's glory will be revealed to you "Day unto Day".

In Christ's love and service,

David Mainse
Host of "100 Huntley Street"

3

Applying this Guide
to Family Devotions

by Lorne Shepherd
100 Huntley Street's Minister to the Family

Many families have good relationships but do not feel close to one another spiritually. Spiritual oneness is important. In fact, if a husband and wife regularly read the Bible together, pray together, and attend church, their chances of divorce drops from one in two marriages to one in four hundred. Family devotions are important!

However, sometimes it is hard to make daily prayer times a habit. Here are some practical steps that will help you to have a spiritual unity in your family.

1. Read the Bible passage and devotional comments with your family or spouse.

2. Each member of the family should discuss something they received from the devotional.

3. During your day, find a scripture that will bless your mate or family members. Do not preach at one another with scriptures.

4. Pray for each of your family member's needs.

5. Start off slowly. Do not feel you have to pray for half an hour. Time with God should be enjoyable. Expand your devotional time as your relationship with God grows.

6. If you have children, sing a children's chorus and tell a parallel real life story that will help them understand the devotional guide's lessons. Make it fun!

Special Note for Singles — during your day, find someone with whom you can share the principles God has given you during your devotional study.

Introduction

"Day Unto Day" is a devotional commentary for the nineties! This book is the sixth of eight volumes which will lead you on a journey through the entire Bible in two years. It's more than a typical daily devotional, and it does not pretend to be an exhaustive commentary. It is designed to lead us deeper and higher into the knowledge of the Almighty God and His Son, the Lord Jesus Christ, through the teaching of the Holy Spirit.

The authors, Jim and Kathy Cantelon with the New Testament and Nizar and Ellen Shaheen, the Old Testament, are uniquely qualified for the task. All have spent many years in the land of the Bible. Let's meet them now:

Jim Cantelon — Jim was the pioneer pastor of the Jerusalem Christian Assembly and remained there for seven years. Prior to going to Jerusalem he served successfully as a Canadian pastor. His practical application of Scripture was well honed as a popular Canadian open-line radio host. In Jerusalem, he continued on radio covering the Middle East regularly, and became deeply involved in the life of the city as a Rotary Club executive. A most unusual congregation of several hundred members was solidly established. His book, "Theology for Non-Theologians" has had excellent reviews in several leading magazines and is published by Macmillan — the fact that this usually "non-religious" publisher would enthusiastically publish his book is a testimony to what is in store for you in your New Testament readings.

Kathy Cantelon — In Jerusalem she was known as Kathy Kennedy for security reasons. Millions knew her through the nightly television news. Kathy's insightful presentation drew a host of loyal viewers. As the daughter of Rev. and Mrs. E. Howard Kerr, and then a pastor's wife and mother of three, her down-to-earth insights, joined with those of Jim, her husband, are treasured.

Nizar Shaheen — Here is an Arab native of Israel, perfectly fluent in Arabic and Hebrew, the languages of the Middle East and of the Old Testament. His ancestral family home is in the village of Cana of Galilee, not far from Nazareth where he was born. In his teen years, he became a boxer. Nizar trained by running from Cana to the sea of Galilee, a distance of fifteen miles. Upon arrival at the sea, he would plunge in, swim vigorously, and then return home. Following his miraculous conversion, he applied that same tremendous drive to reading and re-reading the Bible many times a year. Before long, Nizar was ministering extensively in the churches of Israel and the West Bank, as well as preaching and teaching in various countries at seminars and conferences. His study of the ancient culture of peoples of the Middle East have given him most enlightening insights on Old Testament passages. He studied theology in Brussels for four years and received his degree in theology. Today, Nizar hosts an Arabic television program called, "Light for All the Nations" which reaches the immigrant population from Arab countries here in the west and also covers many countries through "Middle East Television". He is known by many who hear him as "a teacher's teacher".

Ellen Shaheen — It was during her undergraduate work at "The American Institute of Holy Land Studies", located on Mount Zion in Jerusalem, that she met Nizar; she met him near the end of eight months of concentration on Biblical Hebrew, Archeology, and historical Geography of the Holy Land. Their marriage in Cana of Galilee was a traditional Middle Eastern wedding. During the ceremony, when Ellen spoke in the language of Cana, Arabic, and said the words of Ruth, "Thy people shall be my people and thy God, my God", the crowd cheered and took her to their heart. Into her participation with Nizar in the writing of the Old Testament devotional commentaries, she brings a liberal arts degree with a Biblical Studies major. Ellen also brings her upbringing in a minister's home, that of her parents, David and Norma-Jean Mainse. This mother of three active children has spent many hours studying with her husband in the preparation and writing of this fresh material.

David and Norma-Jean Mainse — It was in 1962, at 25 and 22 years of age, that they began regular Christian television programming. Now this work continues with the daily "100 Huntley Street" telecast, the children's productions and the many non-English programs. From the TV programs have been birthed Circle Square Ranches for youth across the continent and overseas missions in many countries. God has obviously blessed David and Norma-Jean. They have taken each of the commentaries of Jim and Kathy, Nizar and Ellen and have written a "Prayer for today" which you can use as a short starter for your daily prayer time. In these short prayers, they have used the term "we" rather than "I" because they pray together and are thinking of all who will participate with them in the *Day Unto Day* readings.

May this work be a great blessing to you as you grow stronger in the Lord through reading His Word and prayer — DAY UNTO DAY!

APRIL

Ruins of a main street of ancient Ephesus,
the city where Timothy pastored.

Special Note: Be sure to write in your request by JUNE 1 for your next volume of *DAY UNTO DAY, the Year Two — Summer* edition. It starts July 1!

Introduction to
The Book of Job

The name of the book comes from its principle character, Job. In the Hebrew text, the name is *iyyob*; however, it is not a Hebrew name. The meaning of Job's name comes from the Arabic root for "return" or "repent" (cf. 42:6). It has been proven by ancient documents that "Job" was an actual common Semitic name. Job was not of Israelite origin. He came from the region east of Canaan in the land of Uz, which was most likely between Edom and Northern Arabia. His friend Eliphaz (2:11) came from Teman, located in Edom, and Elihu was a Buzite (32:2) from northeast Arabia. Job, like his visitors, was a real historical figure who came from an actual place called Uz; the story is not a myth (see James 5:11; Ezekiel 14:13-20).

In the Hebrew Bible, the Book of Job is found within the third section, called "Writings", and in the English Bible, it is the first of the five poetic books (from Job to Song of Solomon) and first in the classification of Wisdom Literature (also Proverbs and Ecclesiastes). It is a splendid example of classical poetry, yet it has a uniqueness all on its own. It has been acclaimed as a literary masterpiece.

The human author is unknown, but we know the divine author is the Holy Spirit who inspired the writer. Ancient Hebrew tradition says the author was Moses, who wrote it while in the desert of Midian (Exodus 2:15); but before it was written down, it had been passed down by oral tradition. Due to its poetic nature, however, many commentators place the writing of the book during the time of Solomon, when the poetic literary form flourished and when the other canonical Wisdom Literature was written.

The date of the actual events recorded in the Book of Job, however, are much earlier. From internal evidence, it appears to be from the patriarchal time period. 1) Job was likely a contemporary of Isaac, Jacob, or Joseph. One of Job's visitors was Bildad the Shuhite (2:11), a son of Shuah, the youngest son of Abraham from Katurah. Abraham had sent him eastward with his brothers so that Isaac might be his sole inheritor in Canaan (Genesis 25:2,6). There are more reasons for an early period: 1) Job, the patriarchal head of his family, was also the priest; 2) wealth is measured in terms of livestock and land; 3) no awareness of the Law of Moses or a Tabernacle; 4) the lack of religious development and progressive revelation; 5) the longevity of Job (140 years); 6) and the reference

Continued on next page

to a certain unit of money used in the time of Jacob (42:11; Genesis 33:19; Joshua 24:32).

More than any other book of the Bible, Job gives insights into the character and work of Satan. He is portrayed as having power, yet it is limited by the Almighty who reigns supreme. Satan knows many things, but he is not all-knowing; he is powerful, but not *all*-powerful like God. Through a philosophical debate between Job and his visitors, several topics are dicussed. These discussions are often very profound and complex. The main theme appears to be the suffering of the righteous and the triumph of faith. The book tries to reconcile the suffering of saints with the goodness of God. The logic and theology of Job's argumentative friends told them that Job must be a great sinner because he was suffering so much, but Job knew their view was untrue. Job was the most righteous man in the east (1:1, 8; 2:3). The book in itself, however, does not contain all the answers to the perplexing questions about suffering. The fuller revelation of God, through Jesus Christ and His Word in the New Testament, answers more fully Job's questions. The purpose of the book seems to be a call for all mankind to greater faith and total consecration of themselves to the Sovereign Lord and Creator of the Universe, whose ways and wisdom are far beyond that of our finite minds. Through the Book of Job, we learn that when we suffer, God has a purpose, and we can be confident that if we remain true to Him, there will be an outcome of blessing.

Key Verse: Job 31:35 *"Oh, that I had one to hear me! Here is my mark. Oh, that the Almighty would answer me...!"*

In Job's final protest of his innocence (chapter 31), he went so far as to call down the wrath of God upon himself if he was not telling the truth (e.g. vv. 8, 10, 22, 40). In so doing, Job made solemn oaths of innocence before his three accusers and before God (compare 1 Kings 8:31-32). He wanted them to know he was undeserving of such treatment and, because of his uprightness, deserved to be justified.

Job asserted his purity of heart and mind, as well as his outward acts of kindness and fairness to all people. He demonstrated that he was a man of high morals and integrity; innocent of lust and adultery (31:1, 9), vain deceit (31: 5), and covetousness (31:7). He did not abuse his wealth and power. His servants were well treated, for he recognized the equality of all mankind (31:15). He was unselfish, generous, and helpful to the poor, the orphan, the widow, and the sojourner. He also recognized that God would one day rise up in defence of those who were oppressed, and he would be answerable to God for how he treated his fellow man; thus he reverently feared the Lord's judgment (31:14, 23).

Job knew that God alone was worthy to be worshipped. He understood that the love of money and putting trust in one's wealth and oneself was equal to idolatry (cf. 1 Tim. 6:10). Therefore, Job abstained from greed and from worshipping his riches, as well as keeping far from the worship of false gods or celestial bodies (31:24-28). He said that such iniquity was worthy of judgment, as it was really the denial of God "who is above" (31:28).

Job continued to defend himself by asserting he was innocent of malice toward those who hated him, and he guarded his tongue so that he would not curse their souls (31:29-30). All his close associates could vouch that Job was a truly good and hospitable man, in whom there was no hypocrisy. Unlike Adam, Job had nothing to hide in his life, but rather lived transparently and openly, so that his righteousness was clearly evident to all. He did not need to fear the close scrutiny of society, nor of God. He did not hide in shame of sin, as did Adam; rather, because of his innocence, he longed to communicate directly with God. His defence was offered up to God as a solemn, legal, and sealed document: "Here is my mark"; but Job lacked a mediator to present his case to God and thus his sadness (31:35). If he had a written indictment of the alleged charges against him, he said he would proudly adorn himself with it and confidently approach God after having been justified (31:35-37). It is only through the redemptive work of Jesus Christ, who turned our sadness into great joy and is ever mediating (interceding) for us before God, that we attain a right standing with God, enabling us to boldly approach Him as His children (cf. Heb. 7:25; 1 Tim. 2:5; 1 John 2:1; Heb 10:19-22).

After Job ended his speech, there was a period of silence. Eliphaz, Bildad, and Zophar did not answer Job, since they believed him to be self-righteous, and their arguments had been exhausted and were of no avail (32:1). The fact that the debate had stopped without an adequate conclusion angered Elihu, a younger man who until this point had been a silent listener. He was apologetic for speaking so boldly to his elders, but he felt compelled by the spirit within him to speak his mind. The Lord chose to use him to bring some light on the discussion and prepare Job for God's answer from out of the whirlwind (38:1ff.). God had given Elihu wisdom which exceeded that of the sages. Wisdom, therefore, is not something gained merely with age; it is a gift of God (James 1:5).

Elihu was angry with Job for questioning God's justice, and thus judging God. He felt Job was seeking only to justify himself and his own honour rather than seeking to uphold God's honour. The Lord Himself later rebuked Job for these very things (cf. 40:8). Elihu was also angry with the three elders for not only failing to answer Job's protests, but for not adequately defending God's honour and condemning Job without proof. Elihu felt that the debaters were narrow-minded, and so with new strategy and fearless determination, he sought to enlighten them; but before he began his discourse, he promised to be impartial, since he was committed to the truth.

Prayer for today: *Father, we ask for Your discernment and wisdom in our dealings with one another this day. Give us loving hearts and Your words of encouragement to lift the weary spirit.*

Read Job 33 &34   *April 2*

Key Verse: Job 33:28 *"He will redeem his soul from going down to the Pit, and his life shall see the light."*

The young man, Elihu, continued his discourse by directing his attention to Job. He respectfully, yet confidently, challenged Job's position, but he also assured Job he had nothing to fear; Elihu would be as Job's "spokesman before God" (33:6), and he sought to justify Job by revealing the truth (33:32).

Job's words concerning his innocence and purity were accurately quoted by Elihu (33:9), but it must be remembered that these words of Job were spoken in defence of the charges laid against him by his three friends and not in denial of a sin nature (cf. 7:21; 13:26). There is, however, a hint of self-righteousness in Job (especially in chapter 31), but Elihu soon proved that Job's complaining attitude toward God and His justice (or, as Job believed, the lack of it) was unrighteous (33:12) and even rebellious (34:37). Job's attitude showed that he lacked wisdom and knowledge (34:35). Elihu argued that it was impossible for God to be unjust and that since He is God and greater than man, man cannot hope to understand all His ways and purposes.

God has only the good of His creation in mind, and contrary to Job's expressed feeling that God is disinterested in mankind, Elihu expressed the truth that "His eyes are on the ways of man, and He sees all his steps" (34:21). God's purpose is to redeem and save mankind from falling into "the Pit", and Elihu gives three means whereby God seeks to save souls and reveal Himself: (1) through dreams and visions (33:15); (2) through chastening with pain and suffering (33:19); and (3) by a righteous messenger or mediator sent by a gracious God to redeem man (33:23-24). This third point was no doubt inspired by God in prophetic anticipation of the Lord Jesus who was that Messenger sent by God, and who Himself became our advocate and was made a ransom (or atonement) for us (1 John 2:1; 1 Tim. 2:5-6; Heb. 7:25).

Job must have been relieved and thrilled to view his suffering in this new light. His suffering was a chastisement, not meted out in proportion to sin, as Eliphaz reasoned (5:17), but a gracious act of God to warn and teach him, so that he might not eventually fall into sin (pride/self-righteousness) and perish in the Pit (33:17-18). Elihu painted a beautiful picture of the joyous restoration God offers (33:25-26), and this surely would have given hope to Job. Elihu pointed out that this restoration must be accompanied by prayer, confession, and repentance, and it involved a restoration of God's righteousness upon man (33:26-27). Truly, without the righteousness of Christ in us, we are as filthy rags before God (Isaiah 64:6, 1John 1:9).

Finally, when Job was given the opportunity to answer Elihu, he had nothing to say. He held his peace and accepted the instruction and wisdom of Elihu (33:31-33). This new insight must have filled Job with shame as he recalled the accusations he made against his gracious and loving God. Elihu continued by quoting Job's complaints against God which actually accused God of being unjust in punishing him, since he was "without transgression" (34:5-6). Elihu went on to argue that God was indeed just and righteous. The Almighty Creator and Ruler of the orderly universe could never pervert justice, for that would mean anarchy, but God is a God of order. He is also a good God, and an impartial, sovereign, and all-knowing Judge over mankind, His creation. In Him all living things find their being (Acts 17:28). If He so desired, He could lift His Spirit from the earth, and all life would perish and return to dust (34:14-15). But God seeks to give man new and more abundant life; that is why He sent His Son Jesus into the world (John 10:10).

Although it is understandable, Job was foolish to question God's benevolent providence, and he was rebellious to question His justice. Job would clap his hands with impatience and indignation against God and speak against Him; this only added to his guilt (34:37). Once again, Elihu gave Job the opportunity to defend his rebelliousness, but Elihu's words of wisdom had again silenced him. This must have been a humbling experience for Job, and he did well to heed the words of young Elihu, who might well have been one of those young men who were once awestruck by Job's presence and no doubt desired to emulate him (29:8). Truly Job once had been an admirable figure and a worthy example, and after his experience of suffering, he would be an even greater example.

Prayer for today: *Father, we come to You today with grateful hearts. Fill us with all spiritual wisdom and understanding, that we might see the good intentions of Your heart even in the midst of adverse circumstances.*

Read Job 35&36   *April 3*

Key Verse: Job 36:10 *"He [God] also opens their ears to instruction, and commands that they turn from iniquity."*

Wise young Elihu confirmed that Job's attitude was one of self-righteousness. Job had criticized God's dealings with him, a righteous man, but he had no grounds to judge God, since he could never be more righteous than God. Elihu reworded Job's sentiments that it made no difference to God whether he had been a sinner or a pious man, and he showed Job this was a wrong view of God's transcendence. Truly, the Lord is higher than our comprehension, and Elihu directed the attention of Job and his friends upward to the heavens which attest to God's majesty and glory. There is nothing that a mere man does (whether wickedness or righteousness) that can change God's most high and glorious position. Therefore, in his administration of justice, God is absolutely impartial and could never have any ulterior motives. A man's wickedness or righteousness, however, does effect the behaviour of one's fellow man (whether negatively or positively, 35:8). For the sake of others, especially our children, we need to be good examples; this greatly pleases God.

Job had questioned God's interest in His creation, since he, a righteous man, felt his prayers went unanswered, while some wicked people were healthy, prosperous, and seemed to go unpunished. Elihu answered by giving reasons why God might not answer prayer. It was certainly not because He is disinterested; on the contrary, He is watchful and hears every cry for help. When one does not receive an immediate answer, it should not make him question God's love and concern or His very existence. Elihu illustrated our Maker's love for us in that He gave us intelligence and wisdom far greater than the animals, and He gave mankind the talent to sing and create music (35:10-11).

The problem of unanswered prayer was not with God but with man. When men are full of pride and "empty talk", God will not regard their pleas (35:12-13). "Empty talk" is selfishly motivited and does not spring from the repentant heart of one desiring to grow more in the knowledge of the Lord. Job's main desire and request to God was for relief from pain, restored wealth, and justice; but the justice Job sought was for God to prove to everyone that he was innocent of any sinful deed, rather than a desire to deepen his relationship and love for God. Elihu assured Job that God would indeed bring justice and thus answer his prayer, but Job must wait patiently, rather than jump to vain conclusions.

Elihu politely requested the continued attention of his audience, since he felt God had given him further truths to teach. Elihu magnified the Almighty God who is truly righteous, just, and all-knowing (36:5). He does punish the wicked and bring justice to the oppressed, as well as continually watch the righteous and exalt them. But if his righteous people suffer affliction, they are to learn from it. If they seek the Lord, He will instruct them and show them where they have fallen short. They may need to be humbled before the Lord, so they might not fall due to pride but rather obey and serve Him as they should. If they do this, the Lord will prosper them; if they do not, they will perish, not having learned from their experience of affliction given to them as a gracious act of the Lord, that they might learn from it and draw closer to Him (36:11-12). These words of Elihu were directed at Job in response to the debated dilemma of his suffering. This knowledge in itself justified Job, for it revealed the purpose of

God in allowing his suffering and disproved the argument of Job's three friends that suffering was solely the result of sin.

If Job had responded to God in the way he should have, his suffering would not have been prolonged and God would have restored him sooner; but Job was filled with complaints and demands for justice, which Elihu called "iniquity". Elihu warned Job that it is better to endure affliction than to turn to iniquity (36:21), for iniquity stirs up God's wrath. Elihu's further words of wisdom reminded Job that God was all-powerful, sovereign, and perfect; no one can accuse Him of wrongdoing. Even in his suffering, Job was reminded to magnify and praise God for all He has done (36:24), even though much of it was a mystery and beyond understanding (36:26). We as believers today must trust God in this way and praise Him despite our circumstances. Though we don't always understand things, we can rest assured that God is in control and has a purpose.

Prayer for today: *Father, You are altogether righteous and just, yet at the same time, merciful and kind. Your love constantly amazes us and delights us. We cast the whole of our cares on You this day, trusting You to lead and direct us in Your good way.*

Read Job 37&38   *April 4*

Key Verse: Job 38:4 *"Where were you when I laid the foundations of the earth? Tell Me, if you have understanding."*

Elihu confessed that when he considers God's greatness and control over the elements of nature, such as thunder and lightning, it causes his heart to tremble (37:1). Elihu taught that God uses natural means (rain, wind, snow, hail) to judge the peoples of the earth and bring correction, as well as to graciously bless the earth with food (36:31; 37:13). When God commands, the natural elements obey (37:12; 36:32), just like when the wind and waves obeyed the voice of the Lord Jesus. These same elements also declare the glory and majesty of God. Mankind seems so small and ignorant compared to God for, "He does great things which we cannot comprehend" (37:5b; Rom. 11:33-36).

Job, who had thought himself to be so very wise and knowledgable, was greatly humbled by Elihu's pointed questions concerning "those wondrous works of Him who is perfect in knowledge" (37:16). Who is man to think that he can tell God what to do? All man's workings are as though they were done in darkness; they amount to nothing compared to the workings of God (37:19-20). God dwells in unapproachable light (1 Tim. 6:16). "God is light and in Him is no darkness at all" (1 John 1:5). Who then was Job that he should even try to face God. Only through Jesus can we approach the Father (cf. Exodus 33:20; John 1:18; 14:5). We are so thankful for this grace, for He has commanded His light to shine in our hearts, and in the face of Jesus we see the glory of God (2 Cor. 4:6; Heb. 1:3). Who was Job to even question God's lovingkindness or argue with Him; after all, "He is excellent in power, in judgment and abundant justice; He does not oppress" (37:23). Elihu's words of wisdom served to teach Job of his ignorance and weakness, that he might submit to God and that his heart would be prepared to receive the words of the Lord.

While Elihu spoke about God's soveriegn control over the wind and clouds, there may well have been a storm brewing to which Elihu drew their attention. Suddenly, the Lord spoke to Job from out of the whirlwind (38:1). Job had longed for God to appear and answer His questions, but he certainly did not expect it in this fashion. God did not gently pat Job on the back and proclaim his innocence and righteousness; rather, He spoke words of reproach which showed Job's ignorance and powerlessness.

God personally continued the teaching that His Spirit had led Elihu to proclaim: His infinite knowledge and wisdom, His greatness and might, and the mysteries and marvels of His creation. The Lord began by challenging Job in order to humble him. God ordered Job, "prepare yourself like a man", which is literally translated as "gird up your loins" (the action of tucking up one's robes in preparation for a wrestling match or physical labour). Could Job match God's great knowledge or deeds? The Almighty asked Job question after question which showed His great, unlimited power and transcendance, as well as demonstrating that man is truly weak, finite, and limited in knowledge, understanding, and wisdom. This confrontation caused Job to be awestruck and dumbfounded, and it must also have driven him to his knees in sorrowful repentance.

Prayer for today: *Thank You, Father, that Your light shines in our hearts and that we have seen Your glory and goodness in the face of Jesus Christ, our Lord and Saviour. Draw us closer to You this day, that we might come to know You better.*

Read Job 39&40   April 5

Key Verse: Job 40:2 *"Shall the one who contends with the Almighty correct Him? He who rebukes God, let him answer it."*

Just as Job was shown to be powerless over nature, so also God made him face the realization of his weakness in controlling animals. Mankind was given dominion over the earth as God's crown of creation, but this was in a very limited sense. As God affirmed, only He has ultimate control over the universe and the natural elements, as well as being sovereign over all creatures, including the animals (chapter 39). He alone has the wisdom to rule. If Job, in his limited knowledge, could not understand these basic facts of nature and the animal kingdom, then how could he be an able ruler or judge? Job was proven totally incompetent, and thus he was humbled.

It is evident in this list of animals and birds that God cares for all His creation. If He provides food and shelter for the animals (Psalm 104:24-29), how much more does He care for mankind, the crown of His creation (Matthew 6:26; 10:29-30)? If the animals have to depend on God for their existence, how much more should we, who have minds to reason and spirits that we might know God? Since Job was in a state of terrible suffering at the time, he needed this confirmation of God's love and care; and even though this divine lecture was a rebuke, it must have still given him great comfort. God wanted Job to lift up His eyes and depend upon Him, as well as witness His glory, wisdom, and love, so that Job might be enlightened (cf. Psalm 36:7-9).

After considering the Lord's greatness, Job no longer felt worthy to approach God as a proud prince, nor could he hope to defend and justify himself before God as he had previously longed to do. Rather, he felt vile and wicked for presuming to judge and contend with God. Once again, God gave Job the opportunity to defend himself, but all he could do was admit defeat and confess that he could not answer God (40:4-5).

God's challenge to Job, however, was not over, for although Job submitted to God, he still had to fully yield to Him by repenting with his whole heart, which involved the recognition that he had sinned by criticizing the Almighty God. It is not a servant's place to tell his master how he should lead, or even give him advice or change his rulings, for in so doing he would be acting as his master's equal or even his superior. God asked Job, "Would you condemn me that you may be justified?" (40:8) As servants of God, our utmost duty is to honour and glorify Him. This cannot be done if we are thinking of ourselves and our own rights. We must decrease and God must increase.

The Lord asked Job, "Have you an arm like God?" (40:9). The arm of the Lord is pictured in the Bible as a mighty force which not only brings judgment but mercifully saves (cf. Isaiah 59:1). Job had confidently expressed that he would overcome what he felt to be God's opposition to his justification. Did he think that with all his arguments and claims of innocence he could save himself? Or could he execute judgment and punishment upon the wicked? If he could, then God would have to bow to him (40:14), but of course that would be far from possible. Only our God's gracious outstretched arm can bring salvation. This outstretched arm reached down to mankind in the person of our Lord Jesus Christ.

Just as Job cannot save his soul, so also he could never hope to save his life from the great beasts that God had created. Only God Himself can confront and control the beasts (40:19). The identification of the "behemoth" (meaning "the beast par excellence") is unknown, but it was not something mythical. Speculation has ranged from a hippopotamus to a dinosaur. We do learn from the text, however, that it was a large, grass-eating land animal that was feared by man. If Job was afraid of the behemoth and unable to confront it, even though it was only a fellow creation of God, how then could he hope to confront God, the creator Himself (cf. 41:10)?

Prayer for today: *Thank You, Lord, for reminding us of Your great desire to care for us in every area of our lives. It is our prayer today that we would "decrease" and You would "increase".*

Read Job 41 &42 *April 6*

Key Verse: Job 42:10 *"And the Lord restored Job's losses when he prayed for his friends. Indeed the Lord gave Job twice as much as he had before."*

Like the behemoth, the "leviathan" was a real animal created by God and its identity is also unkown today; they both may be extinct. Speculation of the leviathan's identity has included the crocodile, a sea dragon/serpent, or a type of dinosaur. The description of the leviathan is probably exaggerated for the sake of poetic imagery and emphasis, which is common to ancient (and modern) middle-eastern poems (e.g. 41:18-21; it's warm breath on top of the cold sea would have resembled smoke). It is clear, however, that just as the behemoth was the most feared beast of the land, leviathan was the most feared of the sea. God used these magnificent and powerful beasts to illustrate His omnipotence, for He, as their creator, had infinitely greater power and strength than they. It would be a foolish act for a mere man to stand against these beasts, just as it would be an even greater folly to stand against God (41:10).

All the animals God described lacked understanding (especially the ostrich. 39:13-17), and it is against their nature to be submissive. Only through force has man been able to tame a few animals. Unlike lowly animals, God gave human beings reason, understanding, choice, and a never-dying soul. We must choose to willingly submit ourselves to God, for He will not use force with us. God could have terrified Job and forcefully, harshly, and very quickly caused him to repent, but He would never do this; rather, He lovingly took much time to speak and reason with Job, so that he might gain a fuller understanding and then choose to love and submit himsélf to God. Although He never directly answered Job's questions concerning the "whys" of his suffering, the fact that God condescended to speak with him showed Job that God was indeed gracious and loving. It was no longer important that he know the "whys" of it all.

When God gave Job the opportunity to respond, Job began by giving mental assent to the fact that God was indeed all-powerful. He confessed his lack of understanding and admitted that God's communication with him had enlightened him to the truth. If Job had never suffered, he would have never come to know God better. Job said, "I have heard of You by the hearing of the ear", meaning that in the past he had only a partial understanding of God. He then went on to say, "but now my eye sees You", meaning he now had a fuller understanding of God. This knowledge of God caused him to see himself as he actually was; not only vile (40:4) but abhorant, for he recognized his sin of rebellion against God, and this led to his sincere repentance and humility before God ("in dust and ashes", 42:6).

The Lord was pleased with Job, but still not pleased with Job's friends, Eliphaz, Bildad, and Zophar, who had falsely accused him. Like Job, they too heard God's words; but unlike Job, they did not see their own sinfulness, nor did they humble themselves and repent before God. Therefore, God addressed Eliphaz (as the eldest, he was the spokesman) and rebuked all three men. Elihu was not mentioned, since he did not share in their folly. The three men had boastfully claimed to understand the purposes of God (cf. Romans 11:34), but in so doing, they judged Job wrongly (without mercy, love, or understanding), and they were harder on Job than was God (cf. Romans 14:4).

Four times in this passage, God referred to Job as "My servant Job" (42:7-8), which was a public justification of his righteousness. It must have thrilled him to hear those words from the Almighty; this made all his suffering worthwhile. Job's righteousness was also reaffirmed in God's remedy for the sinfulness of his three friends, as Job was to mediate for their sacrificial offering, which was a public expression of their repentance (Note: this was before the Law of Moses). Interestingly, Job, whom they had hurt, was told by God to pray for them, since God would now accept his prayers (42:8). In praying for them, Job showed that he forgave them, and this was God's desire. Once Job forgave and prayed for God's blessing upon his friends, then God restored all his losses (42:10). The importance of forgiving those who have hurt you is clear in this passage. When Job's bitterness and anger against his friends was dispelled, God could once again shower Job with blessings. He was restored in every area of his life: friendships, family, possessions, prestige, and a long life; but the greatest blessing was his spiritual restoration. Job's faith had been tested, but he emerged from the fire purer and stronger (cf. Psalm 66:10-12).

The book of Job ends on a triumphant note. Let us remember that Job's sufferings originated as an attack of Satan in a challenge to God (1:9-12), but God was victorious, for although Job questioned God's justice and fell in despair, he never cursed God as Satan had claimed he would. Significantly, Job's deliverance from the hands of Satan and the salvation of Job's friends was marked by the offering of a sacrifice, which typified the future Messianic sacrifice of Jesus Christ. Righteousness can only come through His redemptive work in our lives.

Prayer for today: *Father, it is only in the receiving of Your forgiveness and love that we are able to forgive and love others. We long to know You better this day, that we, in turn, might better serve You.*

Introduction to
The Pastoral Epistles and Philemon

In every sense of the word, what we now know as "The Pastoral Epistles" (1 & 2 Timothy and Titus) are letters. They are not systematic doctrinal dissertations nor are they histories or narratives. In essence, they are fatherly conversations with young proteges — words of wise counsel from a veteran to fresh and vulnerable rookies. The issue (if there *is* one overriding concern) is orthodoxy versus heresy, revealed truth versus fabricated dogma.

Both Timothy and Titus were young men who had been trained by Paul. Timothy had been assigned the difficult pastorate in Ephesus, while Titus the equally problematic pastoral responsibilities in Crete. As Paul's authorized representatives, they were the only ones we know of who receive specific letters of instruction about organizing and stabilizing churches Paul had established.

The basic problem in both areas was the influence of false teachers (1 Tim.4:1-5; 2 Tim.3:1-9; Titus 1:10-16). Paul pulls no punches in his description of these men, and in stark contrast delineates the character of bishops, deacons, and pastors (1 Tim.3:1-13); 4:6-16; 2 Tim.2:1-7, 14-26; Titus 1:5-9). The true pastoral leader must maintain sound doctrine (1 Tim.1:3-7; 6:2c-5; 2 Tim.1:8-14; 2:14-26; 3:14-17; Titus 2:1-10) and commit himself to protecting and teaching orthodox Christianity in his congregations (1 Tim. 2:8-15; 3:14-16). As powerful as his personal ministry gifts may be, the true leader must submit himself to the greater and enduring truth of the Gospel.

The letter to Philemon, on the other hand, is a personal note, (or as some have called it, a "postcard") from Paul to his old friend. It concerns Philemon's runaway slave Onesimus, who, through the providence of God, had come in contact with Paul in Rome. There, Paul had led him to Christ and Onesimus had become not only redeemed but a "brother" to Paul and his former owner. Paul simply wants to inform Philemon about this remarkable turn of events and request that he receive Onesimus back without recrimination. It's a warm, personal letter and there's reason to believe it was well received. Some scholars have suggested that Onesimus later became a much respected Christian bishop.

Read 1 Timothy 1 — April 7

Key Verse: 1 Timothy 1:15 *"This is a faithful saying and worthy of all acceptance, that Christ Jesus came into the world to save sinners, of whom I am chief."*

Paul is quoting something he, and presumably Timothy, have both memorized — perhaps it's part of an early Christian creed or hymn: "Christ Jesus came into the world to save sinners." This "saying", Paul says, is "faithful and worthy of all acceptance." You can trust it.

Let's look at its component parts. The subject of the saying is Christ Jesus. The word "Christ" means "the anointed one", or, in the Jewish context, "the Messiah". To this day in Israel, Jewish believers refer to Jesus as "Yeshua ha Meshiach" — He is the One spoken of by Isaiah as "Wonderful, Counselor, Mighty God, Everlasting Father, Prince of Peace" (Is.9:6). The verb "came" speaks of movement, in this case "into the world", from the eternal dimension into and onto our temporal earth (see Philippians 2:5-11). This movement is called "incarnation" — God becoming flesh and dwelling among us (John 1:14). The infinitive "to save" describes the purpose of the incarnation. Mankind was terminally diseased and unholy, without hope and eternally lost, apart from some redemptive act on God's part. That's why God sent His Son. The blood He shed on Calvary's cross once and for all atoned for our sin. All we must do is confess our need and put our trust in Him.

The final words of the sentence, "of whom I am chief", tell us that Paul is not speaking merely in theoretical terms. He recognizes his need of salvation, so much so that he sees himself as chief of sinners. There's no rationalizing of behaviour here. Rather, there's a strong acknowledgement that "all have sinned and fallen short of the glory of God."

Prayer for today: *Thank You, Father, that we who were once afar off have been brought near by the blood of Christ. We come to you with grateful hearts for your mercy and great love, for even when we were dead in our transgressions, You made us alive together with Christ.*

Read 1 Timothy 2 — April 8

Key Verse: 1 Timothy 2:1,2 *"Therefore I exhort first of all that supplications, prayers, intercessions, and giving of thanks be made for all men, for kings and all who are in authority, that we may lead a quiet and peaceable life in all godliness and reverence."*

In the world of Paul's day, the common thing was to pray *to* emperors. Many Caesars of that time erected statues of themselves and required, by law, worship from their people. To pray *for* an emperor, therefore, was a radical and dangerous notion.

There were two critical implications in praying for "kings and all who are in authority": 1) it implied that kings were not deities, but human, and 2) there was some higher Deity to whom even this world's leaders were subject and accountable. What's more, in terms of verse four, these men were just as much in need of salvation as anyone else.

Paul had a high view of prayer. He saw it as a central aspect, both in the life of the church and in the life of nations. He linked it with decisions made "at the top" which would produce "a quiet and peaceable life" in everyday experience. Whether the nation's leaders were believers themselves apparently was not the issue. The issue was that a nation's welfare was inextricably tied to the prayerfulness or unprayerfulness of the church.

There's a subtlety in praying for leaders. We don't always like them or agree with their policies, but we're to pray for the leader, not for his politics. We're to pray, "Thy will be done on earth..." In other words, we pray that *God's* agenda will be fulfilled — not *our* agenda, not the leader's agenda, but *God's*. We're to pray for justice and righteousness. And if *we* live justly and righteously, we will discover eventually that "righteousness exalts a nation".

Prayer for today: *Father, in accordance with Your Word, we pray for the leaders of our country and all who are in positions of authority, that we may lead quiet and peaceable lives in all godliness and reverence. We pray both for their salvation and that You would direct them in leadership. May Your will be done on earth as it is in heaven.*

Read 1 Timothy 3 *April 9*

Key Verse: 1 Timothy 3:16 *"And without controversy great is the mystery of godliness: God was manifested in the flesh, justified in the Spirit, seen by angels, preached among the Gentiles, believed on in the world, received up in glory."*

What Paul is about to say is "without controversy" or "beyond all question" (NIV). He is about to quote part of what the majority of Bible commentators see as an early Christian hymn or liturgical creed. We don't know the full text of the hymn, so we cannot speculate as to context. What we do know is that these six statements, precisely and poetically written as they are, present solid, orthodox theology.

(1) "God was manifested in the flesh". Foundational to Christian theology is the incarnation: God in the flesh, in human nature, in human form. Jesus Christ was born in the flesh and resurrected in the flesh, fully God and fully man.

(2) "justified ['vindicated', NIV] in the Spirit" — Jesus was "led by the Spirit" into the wilderness to be tested, and He triumphed over Satan "in the power of the Spirit" (Lk.4:1-4). Then, in Paul's words, Jesus, "through the Spirit of holiness was declared with power to be the Son of God by His resurrection from the dead..." (Rom.1:4 NIV). The Holy Spirit fully established Jesus' credentials as Son of God and Son of Man.

(3) "seen by angels". Not only did angels witness Jesus' resurrection and ascension, but they also witnessed His exaltation (Phil.2:9-10). Even the evil powers of darkness bore witness to this (Col.2:15). He ascended into Heaven and there was revealed in His full splendor, superior to the angelic host, "a priest forever, in the order of Melchizedek" (Heb.1-5:10).

(4) "preached among the Gentiles". Jesus was Jewish; so were the apostles. He fulfilled Jewish Law and the apostles wrote a Gospel founded on "the Law and the Prophets". Paul was the first full-time missionary to the Gentiles, and so effective was his, and subsequent, missionary efforts that Jesus became,

(5) "believed on in the world" — so much so that Gentile believers far outweigh Jewish believers numerically. In every sense of the word, the central message of Judaism — "Messiah" — has become a "light" to the nations.

(6) "received up in glory". It's only speculation to presume to know why reference to Christ's ascension is made at this point, apparently out of chronological order. However, my instinct is this: one of the most glorious themes of Christianity, both then and now, is that of the Lamb of God triumphantly and majestically taking His place at the right hand of God the Father. Ultimately, our theology bows its knee to the heavenly mystery — the ultimate reality: Christ the king, forever, world without end.

Prayer for today: *Lord, we marvel at Your flawless wisdom and rejoice in the grace by which we stand. We thank You for the overwhelming assurance that Jesus, our Lord and King, reigns supreme over all.*

Read 1 Timothy 4 *April 10*

Key Verse: 1 Timothy 4:16 *"Take heed to yourself and to the doctrine. Continue in them, for in doing this you will save both yourself and those who hear you."*

As stated in the introduction, these letters were written by Paul to Timothy when Timothy was less than twenty-five years old and pastoring the church in Ephesus. Being young in the ministry, then as now, could be a problem. There were lots of older "saints" in the congregation who thought they knew more than "the kid in the pulpit". This is why Paul says, "Don't let anyone look down on you because you are young" (v.12- NIV). Then he goes on to give this young pastor some good fatherly advice.

It's a pretty tall order. Paul tells Timothy to "set an example" in what he says — in lifestyle, in seeking the best for others, in faith, and in morality (v.12b). Self-discipline, consistency and faithfulness are to characterize this youthful religious leader. He's to be someone no one can fault and everyone can emulate. The question is, how?

Perhaps the answer is singleness of purpose. Timothy is instructed to focus on his gift (v.14) and expend his energies on "public reading of Scripture", and "preaching and teaching" (v.13). He is to give himself "wholly to them" (v.15) in a visible and accountable way. That way he'll stay on track.

Singleness of purpose, follow-through, and accountability — these are the key ingredients, for both young and old, to make one's life count for God. It's the old story of practising what you preach.

Prayer for today: *Father, as we look at our Lord Jesus' ministry on earth, we see the perfect example of "practising what you preach". Today we grasp hold of the promise Your Word holds out to us — if we ourselves take heed to the doctrine and "be not just hearers of the Word but doers also", we will experience all the benefits of salvation, and so will those who hear and watch us.*

Read 1 Timothy 5 *April 11*

Key Verse: 1 Timothy 5:8 *"But if anyone does not provide for his own, and especially for those of his own household, he has denied the faith and is worse than an unbeliever."*

In my personal notes, I've entitled verses 4 and 8, "Priorities in Christian living". Being religious can be very pleasurable and self-fulfilling. It can appeal attractively to our innate predisposition to self-righteousness and pride. It can even be fun. But it can also totally miss the point. Who are we trying to impress in our religiosity? Ourselves? Our neighbour? God? It's easy to please ourselves — especially by comparing ourselves favourably to "ungodly" friends and relatives. It's even easy to impress our neighbours — most of us are sure to notice someone's fervent piety — but how does one move God?

Jesus demonstrated in so many instances that religion can be self-serving and totally out of line with God's will and pleasure. In fact, on one occasion He referred to the most commitedly religious of His day as "whited sepulchres". Paul (1 Cor.13) made it very clear that even spiritual giftedness was obnoxious to God ("clashing cymbols") if there was no prior commitment to love.

That's why our profession of faith is hollow if we are not caring for our own family. We can pray and celebrate faith all we want, but it's obnoxious if God, who sees all, knows we're neglecting the needs of our parents. God is no fool; He can't be conned.

James, Jesus' half-brother, put it this way, "Pure and undefiled religion before God and the Father is this: to visit orphans and widows in their trouble..." (Jas.1:27). Let your hands and feet do the talking!

Prayer for today: Father, You have said that You seek for worshippers who will worship You in spirit and truth. We ask that You give us wisdom and understanding to rightfully divide the Word of truth, that we might please You in all our relationships, especially those in our own families.

Read 1 Timothy 6   *April 12*

Key Verse: 1 Timothy 6:6 *"Now godliness with contentment is great gain."*

This key verse must be read in the context of verses 3-10. In 3-5 Paul refers to false teachers who promote their own words over the "wholesome words...of our Lord Jesus Christ". These words of Christ promote "godliness", but the words of the false teachers produce "envy, strife, reviling, evil suspicions..." Their "wranglings" come from a "corrupt mind", totally bankrupt of truth. Their motivation is simply described: money — they suppose that "godliness is a means of gain."

In verses 9 and 10, Paul describes the peril of those "who desire to be rich" (and the context is that of seeking gain through ministry). Eagerness for money has led some from near-truth to half-truth to no truth — and brought upon themselves "many griefs". They may have achieved their financial goals, but their relationships have soured and their lives are empty. Covetousness, like pride, is a spiritual cancer that voraciously destroys life from the inside; it rules and it kills.

The only cure for this cancer is contentment. Francis Shaeffer, in his book "True Spirituality", says that covetousness is a lack of "proper contentment". To the extent that we are content, we are free.

Add contentment to godliness and you've got a powerful combination. Trusting God, obeying His Word, and loving (rather than envying) your neighbour makes you spiritually and morally indestructible. It's the only "gain" worth pursuing.

Prayer for today: *Father, we thank and praise You for the abundance of Your household. Thank You for bringing to our remembrance the fact that we have nothing to fear. You indeed supply all our needs according to Your riches in glory by Christ Jesus.*

Read 2 Timothy 1   *April 13*

Key Verse: 2 Timothy 1:7 *"For God did not give us a spirit of timidity, but a spirit of power, of love and of self-discipline" (NIV).*

Timothy was a very young pastor with a very important position, that of pastoring the vital and large church in Ephesus. He was also having a very tough time. There were various power-blocs in the church who were trying to gain control of the congregation in Paul's absence. They resented Paul's choice of Timothy as pastor and did everything they could to discredit and intimidate the young man.

Apparently they were succeeding. Timothy was so intimidated that he had actually become "ashamed" as a preacher and had even become "ashamed" of Paul (see v.8 — part of the intimidation tactic was to question Paul's integrity: some of them ridiculed his continual predisposition to being thrown in jail — see v.12, 15, 16, 2:9, 4:16). Timothy's ministry had become characterized by a spirit of "timidity". The flame of his calling had almost died — there was a mere whisper of smoke where a fire had once burned.

That's why paul reminds Timothy to "fan into flame the gift of God" which is in him (v.6 — NIV). This is to be more than mere bravado; rather it's to be done in the context of the "spirit" God has given him.

God has given him the "power" to be bold and assertive in preaching. He has given him the "love" to be effective in pastoring, and He has given him the capability to be "self-disciplined". With these "givens" comes responsibility — and Paul expects Timothy to get out of his shell and back into battle.

Prayer for today: *Thank You, Father, that You have not left us alone or powerless, but You have given the Holy Spirit to dwell in us, empowering us with Your divine love and control. Teach us to continually draw upon this great and limitless source within us.*

Read 2 Timothy 2 April 14

Key Verse: 2 Timothy 2:15 *"Be diligent to present yourself approved to God, a worker who does not need to be ashamed, rightly dividing the word of truth."*

Let us remember the context here: Paul is writing to one of his spiritual "sons" who is having a tough time in his first pastorate. All of us who read the letter can benefit from it as well — but the prior recipient was Timothy, a young and inexperienced preacher, teacher, and pastor.

I like the way the NIV puts it, "Do your best to present yourself to God as one approved, a workman who does not need to be ashamed and who correctly handles the word of truth." There should be no misunderstanding here: Paul would be the first to say we are "justified by faith", that is, our standing in God's eyes is dependent on our faith in the work of Christ on Calvary. However, in the context, Timothy's "justification" is a given — Paul simply wants Timothy to act as an "approved" believer should act. He wants Timothy's life, and especially his work, to reflect his faith.

A vital part of Timothy's work was the correct handling of "the word of truth". God's word is to be treated with respect and taken seriously (see 3:16). This means, among other things, avoiding the temptation of what theologians call "isogesis" — which simply means reading "into" the text (as contrasted to "exegesis": reading "out of" the text). From time to time, all of us would like to make Scripture say what we want it to say. This can easily be done if we isolate the text from its context.

That is why context is so important. Before reading a doctrine into the text, we must weigh it against what we know to be true from the broader doctrines of the entire Bible. Our subjective view must be tempered by the objective truth of the "whole counsel of God". Without this, we do what so many historically have done — mishandle the Word and fall into error.

Prayer for today: Thank You, Father, for Your precious, life-giving Word, which enlightens, corrects, instructs, and guides us daily. We delight in the assurance that You are indeed faithful to give us our daily bread.

Read 2 Timothy 3   *April 15*

Key Verse: 2 Timothy 3:14,15 *"But as for you, continue in what you have learned and have become convinced of, because you know those from whom you learned it, and how from infancy you have known the holy Scriptures, which are able to make you wise for salvation through faith in Christ Jesus." (NIV)*

Paul now turns his attention to the "last days". He has a bleak outlook: "People will be lovers of themselves, lovers of money, boastful, proud, abusive, disobedient to their parents, ungrateful, unholy, without love, unforgiving, slanderous, without self-control, brutal, not lovers of the good, treacherous, rash, conceited, lovers of pleasure rather than lovers of God..." (vv.2-4). Ironically, these self-absorbed people will at the same time be religious, "having a form of godliness" (v.5). They will also have inquiring minds, "always learning" (v.7); but their "godliness" will lack ("deny") power, and their "learning" will lack ("never able to acknowledge") truth. In other words, they will be "spiritual" but self-deceived.

So how does one avoid self-deception in religion? Paul tells Timothy, "continue in what you have learned and have become convinced of..." Timothy has been trained in sound doctrine from his childhood (1:5). His mother Lois and his grandmother Eunice were godly women who had given Timothy a solid scriptural basis for faith. Paul continued training Timothy until he was fit (in Paul's view) to be given the pastorate in Ephesus. Timothy has a sure foundation: a scriptural education taught by trustworthy teachers ("You know those from whom you learned it"). Now, as life's experience adds to his education, it is filtered and tempered by "the holy Scriptures". The subjective is balanced by the objective.

Scripture does much more than address felt needs. It meets *real* needs. That's why submitting oneself to the study of Scripture means being taught, rebuked, corrected, and trained in righteousness (v.16). It will "bless" us once in a while too, but mainly it will equip us for "every good work" (v.17).

Prayer for today: *Father, we praise You and thank You for the sufficient grace and the many opportunities to put into practice what You have taught us this day.*

Read 2 Timothy 4   *April 16*

Key Verse: 2 Timothy 4:7 *"I have fought the good fight, I have finished the race, I have kept the faith."*

When someone dies, we usually manage to say something good about him. Sometimes we really have to stretch to find something positive, but it's a rare eulogy indeed that doesn't end on an upbeat. And, if we were to look at these eulogies from the point of view of the departed, we might see them totally embarrassed by all the plaudits. In fact, many people about to die will say that if they had it to do all over again, they'd do a lot of things differently.

How refreshing, then, to see an old apostle look back and say, "I did a good job. I'm pleased with my performance. I'm happy with my life." That's essentially what Paul says in the key verse.

He uses athletic imagery. Like a boxer, he's fought "a good fight". Like a runner, he's "finished the race" — probably a marathon and steeplechase combined! In the context of athletic games, he has "kept the faith" or "kept [his] pledge to keep the rules". He was true to the faith in terms of both obeying it and communicating it. And you can be sure *"the* faith", as an objective reality, took precedence over his personal experience of faith as a subjective reality. He had his ups and downs, but "the faith" never wavered. Paul was true to the faith, because the faith was true to him. Indeed, Jesus, "the righteous judge", had proven to be all He said He would be.

"Fighting" meant involvement, with all its cuts and bruises. "Finishing" meant commitment — follow-through, with all its good and bad times. "Keeping" meant faithfulness, with all its cost. In every sense of the word, Paul was a "mature" Christian. He had a hope, and he stuck to his goal. Now he is about to pass the relay baton on to younger men.

Prayer for today: *Father, as we read of Paul's "good fight", the desire to "run the race" and "fight the good fight" burns afresh in our own hearts. Your Word has renewed us, and it calls us once again to press on to what lies ahead.*

Introduction to
The Psalms

The Book of Psalms, often referred to as the "Psalter", is the longest and the central book of the Bible. It is truly the heart of the whole Bible and one of the most popular books. In it we find lovely hymns, poems, and petitions, the majority of which are directed to God. There is a wide range of topics, situations, and moods which make it relevant to every person in every generation, and it is especially meaningful for personal devotions, since it is food for the soul and also serves as a guide for our own petitions and praise to the Lord. The psalms sooth the troubled soul, strengthen, guide, help, encourage, and give hope to the believer. Much of the material is very simple and yet profound.

The various psalms were written over a long period of time. The earliest is attributed to Moses (Psalm 90) and the later psalms were post-exilic (i.e. after the return from the Babylonian captivity, the time of Ezra and Nehemiah). As such, they have a wide range of audiences, occasions, and subjects. King David wrote the majority of the psalms, and some were composed by Asaph, Moses, Solomon, Heman, Ethan, and the sons of Korah. Other psalms remain anonymous but were likely also composed by David. They were all pious men who had experienced a close and personal relationship with God, and we can learn much from their varied experiences of life and God's revelation to them. God is portrayed as the Sovereign King of the world who is compassionate and who delivers His people from distress. A common theme is "His mercy endures forever", something for which He is to receive praise forever. Although many of the psalms are nationalistic, there is a repeated invitation for all God's creation to praise and worship Him, both Jew and Gentile alike.

When these 150 psalms were compiled, the book came to be known in the Hebrew as Tehillim, "Praises", since the praise hymns are the most outstanding and almost all the psalms contain some note of praise to the Lord. The English name of "Psalms" comes from the Greek, which implies poems that are sung and accompanied by stringed instruments. The Hebrew word which corresponds to it is "mizmor", which occurs in the title of fifty-seven psalms. This and other Hebrew words are often found in the titles that precede the various psalms, and they designate the specific type of musical accompaniment, rhythm, or melody for the hymn. King

Continued on next page

Continuation of
The Psalms

David and others wrote many of the psalms for the expressed purpose of congregational and liturgical worship, which was led by the Levites at the Lord's House.

The Book of Psalms is divided into five smaller books. Jewish tradition says that this was done so that it might be structured like the five books of Moses and reflect the Israelite's appreciation for God's gift of the Law. The book has many expressions of praise to the Lord for giving the Law, His Word (e.g. all of Psalm 119).

The psalms are usually classified according to their subjects, such as penitential psalms, ascrostic (alphabetic) psalms, historical psalms, pilgrim psalms, and of course, praise psalms. Another very important classification that should not be overlooked is the Messianic psalms, which are those that specifically and prophetically refer to our Lord Jesus' life, ministry, and reign. Considering its many Messianic prophecies, it is justifiable to say that the Book of Psalms centres around Jesus, the great Messiah and King.

Key Verse: Psalm 2:12b *"Blessed are all those who put their trust in Him."*

Psalm 1 serves as an introduction to the whole book of Psalms, as it clearly expounds the book's basic underlying message: happiness, blessedness, and life come to the righteous who walk in the ways of the Lord; sadness, destruction, and death come to the ungodly who do not know the Lord. This first psalm contrasts these two very different ways of life, leading to two opposite destinies. The book of Psalms begins with a beatitude, "blessed is the man", and firstly describes the negative side — what the righteous man does not do. He does not walk in the counsel of the ungodly, meaning he does **not** adopt their standards or principles of life. He does not stand in the path of sinners, meaning he does not practice their evil deeds. He does not sit in the seat of the scornful, meaning he does not fellowship with those who scorn God. The righteous man's life, then, is one of total separation from that which is worldly and is a life of no compromise.

On the positive side, what the righteous man **does** do is continually delight in and meditate on the law of the Lord, that is the whole divinely revealed Word of God (1:2). To meditate on it is not only to read it but to ponder upon and discuss it. Pondering takes time, and it pleases God when we take time with Him and His Holy Word. It is like our daily food; we need it regularly to keep strong. As a result, the righteous man becomes like a tree that God has planted for the purpose of bearing fruit and blessing others. If a believer wants to have a more productive and consistent life, a life of bringing others into the kingdom of God (bearing fruit), his roots must be tapped into the Source of strength by meditating daily on God's Word (cf. Jeremiah 17:8; Isaiah 58:11). The godly are firmly rooted, watched over, and cared for by God (He "knows the way of the righteous"), but the ungodly are blown away like chaff, having no part in the vindication of the righteous, and destruction awaits them (1:6).

Psalm 2 deals with the two different destinies of nations and ends with a beatitude (a blessing) for those who put their trust in the Lord. It is the first of the Messianic psalms, for although the immediate context was likely an actual historical uprising against the coronation of David or Solomon as Israel's divinely anointed king, divine inspiration revealed that it is in essence about God's Anointed Messiah Jesus. The words of this psalm affirm Christ's deity (2:7) and foretell of the opposition to His Kingship, as well as foretelling of His triumph and millenial reign (cf. Acts 4:25-27).

The nations, in deliberate enmity, rise up against God's Anointed (the Messiah), and conspire together to overthrow Him. It is futile and absolute foolishness to attempt to overthrow God's plan and purpose, and God Himself laughs at man's ridiculous folly and ignorance. Soon, however, His laughter turns to wrath, and He puts them in derision and distress. He proclaims that the Anointed One is His begotten Son whose kingdom will indeed be established. He will conquer, have universal reign, and bring justice to the whole earth (cf. Romans 1:18; 2 Thessalonians 2:8-13; Hebrews 1:2-3). God issues a warning to the rebellious nations, for it is not His desire that they perish (cf. Ezekiel 33:11), but unless they repent, "be wise", "serve the Lord with fear", and "kiss the Son" (pay Him homage and give the respect and honour due Him, which includes obedience and submission), they will indeed come to national destruction (2:10-11). Righteousness, however, exalts a nation, and blessed is the nation whose God is the Lord.

Psalm 3 illustrates well the peaceful trust one can have in the Lord, even in the face of adversity. It was this kind of trust that brought David through the very difficult and painful situation of his son Absalom rebelling against Him (2 Samuel 15:13-14, 30). The people had gossiped that David did not have the help of God (3:2), likely because of his sin with Bathsheba, but David had sincerely repented and God accepted his supplication (3:4). His faith and confidence could not be shaken, for God was his "shield" of protection, his "glory" to restore his dignity, and the "One who lifts up" his head to give him courage and strength (3:3). David was confident that the Lord had heard his prayer of faith. At this point in the psalm, we read the word "selah", a musical notation which is likely a pause for the sake of meditation, possibly during a musical interlude.

God did indeed hear and intervene in this seemingly hopeless situation. David's trust in God was based upon God's faithfulness. He knew that God had chosen him as the anointed king and had promised him an eternal dynasty. His knowledge of God's lovingkindness and mercy caused him to sleep in peace, even though his enemies were seeking his death. He awoke like a new man; God had sustained him, and he had no fear. With faith, David could speak as though the salvation of the Lord had already been accomplished, for he knew that God would bless his people.

Prayer for today: *Thank You, Lord, for Your Word which encourages our hearts as we meditate on it day and night. What a blessing it is to place our trust in You, as did David. Oh for grace to trust You more!*

Key Verse: Psalm 5:12 *"For You, O Lord, will bless the righteous; with favor You will surround him as with a shield."*

From these psalms we learn that even though distressful situations surround the godly, they may rest assured that God is watching over them. The historical circumstance of **Psalm 4** is likely the same as Psalm 3, when Absalom was in rebellion against his father David. With trust and serenity, David appeals to God for deliverance. He has confidence that God will deliver him, since God had proven himself in the past (4:1). David admonishes his adversaries, who had slandered his reputation, to meditate or listen to their consciences before they sleep (as should we all), so that they might not sin (4:4; cf. Ephesians 4:26). They should realize that fighting against King David, the one whom the Lord had chosen and anointed, was to fight against God Himself and was therefore futile. It is no wonder David was calm and confident, saying, "The Lord will hear when I call to Him "(4:3). Unlike the pessimistic people around him, David's trust in God gave him great gladness of heart, as well as peace of mind. In this evening prayer, David acknowledges that God alone is his safety (not his bodyguard or army), and so he can sleep without worrying and have true rest.

In **Psalm 5**, David is once again surrounded by foes, but he was a man of prayer, praying in the evening (Psalm 4) and now also in the morning. Rather than being downcast because of his grim circumstances, David looks to the Lord for strength and guidance. It is only by looking to God that one can live above the circumstances, not under them, and "keep the victory". David had warned his adversaries to repent and trust in God (4:4-5). It appears, however, that his words went unheeded, for his foes continued in their wickedness. So David prays in this psalm that God will destroy those violent, lying, rebellious workers of iniquity. David knew that his Most Holy God hated sin and must punish sinners, so he declares that God would destroy them (5:6). Continuing his prayer, David shows the sharp contrast between the wicked and the righteous. While his foes are working iniquity, he is reverently worshipping the Lord and committing his ways to Him. Those who rebel against God are pronounced guilty, made to fall in defeat, and cast out (5:10); but the godly are full of joy, blessed, and protected by His mighty arm, as though surrounded by a shield. The righteous have the greatest weapon — they can turn to the Lord in prayer. What then is there to fear?

In **Psalm 6**, we see that David is in deeper distress than in any of the preceding psalms. There were many distressing events in David's life (2 Samuel records many), including his own sinful deeds (e.g. with Bathsheba), and this is a psalm of repentance. Clearly, David is suffering, possibly with a life-threatening sickness, but his cry for mercy comes out of the suffering of his soul. He recognizes the chastisement of God as the reason for his suffering. Unlike Job, he does not insist upon his innocence, nor does he deny his sin; he merely admits his weakness and throws himself upon God's mercy (6:2). He prays that God's chastisement will not lead to his death, and He reasons with God to deliver him so he might live to praise Him (6:5).

With poetic exaggeration, David expresses his great grief (in recognition of his sin), which causes him to groan and weep profusely (6:6). Like Job, his enemies' insults added to his suffering and grief (6:7). But suddenly, there is a change in David's tone (6:8) as he seems to have regained his strength and boldness. David loudly rebukes his enemies, for he is now confident that the Lord has heard his supplication (6:9).

Prayer for today: *You are there, dear Lord, in our times of trouble, and You hear the cry of the righteous. Thank You for the divine protection and blessings You are so willing to give to those who trust You.*

Read Psalms 7&8   *April 19*

Key Verse: Psalm 8:1 *"O Lord, our Lord, how excellent [majestic] is Your name in all the earth."*

In **Psalm 7**, David is under very strong persecution, which is indicated by the image of the lion that has the strength to tear him into pieces, yet David still trusts in the Lord. The title of the psalm indicates that slanderous words had been spoken against David by Cush, a Benjamite. He was likely a companion or relative of King Saul, also a Benjamite, who was attempting to kill David at the time. It appears that Cush was eager to injure David, and this intensifies David's struggle for survival. It was at this time that David and his band of outlaws were hiding in the wilderness under God's protection.

David, however, was innocent of wrongdoing against Saul, both when they were friends and when David was in exile. It is probable that David is remembering the two occasions when he had the chance to kill Saul, his enemy, but he mercifully spared his life (see 1 Samuel 24:12, 13 and 26:18). David felt confident that he was innocent and had maintained his integrity, and so he cries out to God in the form of an oath, wherein he was willing to accept any punishment if he had done wrong (7:3-5). David urgently called upon God

(7:6), not only to judge the wicked but to judge him as well (7:8). Like David, the righteous need not fear the judgment and scrutiny of God, for God Himself is their defense and Righteous Judge who is most just and "saves the upright in heart" (7:10).

David did not retaliate for the slanderous words hurled against him; rather, he left the retribution to the Lord (cf. Romans 12:19), confident that God's wrath, like the most sophisticated weapons of warfare, will come daily against the wicked (7:11-13). David was also confident that the one who sinfully slandered him would give birth to falsehood (compare James 1:15) and that God would see to it that the trouble he made for him would return on his own head (7:14-16; e.g. Haman, Esther 7:7-10). Upon considering God's faithfulness to the righteous, David bursts forth with praise to the Lord Most High (7:17).

Psalm 8 starts and ends with the same verse, glorifying the Lord whose matchless, majestic, and beautiful name (Yahweh) is Sovereign over all the earth. David may have written this joyous hymn of praise to God while he was a shepherd boy, having much time in the open fields to ponder the greatness of God. As he looked up into the night sky over the rolling hills around Bethlehem, he was filled with awe and wonder at the beauty of the starry heavens which he perceived as clearly reflecting God's glory (19:1). Such majesty demanded praise for the Creator. Because of his young age, David may have been referring to himself when he sang, "Out of the mouth of babes and infants You have ordained strength [or 'praise']" (8:2). Jesus Christ quoted this verse as referring to Himself (Matthew 21:16). In praising God, we receive divine strength, and David discovered this from personal experience: He was enabled by God to kill both a vicious bear and a lion (1 Samuel 17:34-37). When we praise God, the enemy is silenced; Satan's roar cannot be heard.

The wonder of God's greatness and glory in creation, especially in the great expanse above, caused David to marvel at God's condescension to even consider mankind, who is comparatively so small and insignificant. "What is man that You are mindful of him, and the son of man that You visit [attentively and gracefully care for] him?" (8:4). David was overcome with a feeling of unworthiness and inferiority before the majesty of God. Compared to God, who is perfect, has all authority, and is the Source of being, man seems so weak, imperfect, finite, and even filthy; yet man had been honoured by God by giving him dominion (responsibility as a steward) over all His creation, simply because man had been made in His spiritual image and given a moral sense. Man was therefore the crown

37

of God's creation. We are of great value to God and hold a special place in His heart, for He loves all mankind, and even before the foundation of the world, He provided redemption for us. Because of God's love and care, He visited man through the incarnation of Jesus Christ. Christ's visitation was the ultimate in divine condescension, which still causes us to marvel (see Hebrews 2:5-9). God came in the flesh and, in the fullest meaning of Psalm 8:6, all things have been put under His feet (1 Corinthians 15:27).

Prayer for today: *Our spirits soar in praise to You, oh Lord, when we consider Your majesty and power over all creation, as well as Your personal love for each one of us. We cannot understand such great love, but we accept it and return it.*

Read Psalms 9 &10   *April 20*

Key Verse: Psalm 9:9 *"The Lord also will be a refuge for the oppressed, a refuge in times of trouble."*

Psalm 9 and 10 are closely related. They were originally considered as one unit in the early manuscripts. Both speak of the judgment of God upon the wicked and God's help to the poor and oppressed. Psalm 9 is more of a thanksgiving prayer for victory over the wicked, and Psalm 10 is a prayer against the wicked who are deserving of punishment.

A grateful heart will always find a way to express that gratitude. In **Psalm 9**, King David began his song by uttering beautiful words of praise to God. The historical reason for David's personal joy comes from his thankfulness to God for delivering him from his enemies, giving him victory in battle, vindicating him, and establishing his kingship in Israel. God's intervention in taking up the cause of David proved that he had truth and righteousness on his side (9:4). David also experienced spiritual joy because of God's continuous righteous judgment of the wicked and His protection from the oppression of the enemy (9:9). God was truly his refuge in times of trouble. Therefore, David's joy compelled him to proclaim God's marvelous deeds and sing glad praises unto Him (9:1-2). There was also a collective (national) joy among the people of God, so David encouraged the whole congregation of Israel to sing His praises and be witnesses to all people by declaring God's marvelous deeds (9:11; 96:3, 10).

All these good things are available to those who "know" God's Name and "seek" Him (9:10). Those who know God's Name are those who have an intimate relationship with Him, and because they know

38

Him, they seek, serve, and obey Him with their whole hearts. In that precious and Most Holy Name, they can put their trust. We now know that Name is Jesus, the Name above all names, by which we must be saved (Philippians 2:9; Acts 4:12).

In **Psalm 10**, David's prayer is enlarged from being more personal to one that included the hope and faith of the whole nation. David was perplexed because of God's seeming disinterest or indifference regarding the oppression from the wicked. As it was with Job, David's faith and committment to God was being tested.

Wicked men were oppressing the poor and helpless, who in turn cried out to God for salvation. According to the psalmist, all the offenses the evil men did were rooted in their greed and pride. They behaved as though God did not exist (10:4), and even if He did, they believed He did not see them (10:11); so they thought they could get away unpunished for their wrongdoings (10:6, 13). How wrong these wicked people would be proven when they felt the sting of God's wrath! The psalm that began on a note of distress and defeat radically changes to a note of confidence and victory as David prays with faith that God would "arise" to bring judgment and justice (10:12). David rightly knew that God was omniscient: He does indeed see every wrongdoing and observes the plight of the helpless and oppressed (10:14).

The Helper of the oppressed is also the Great King who reigns forever. He will make all things right. These descriptive verses about "the evil man" seem to prophetically anticipate the evil deeds of the Antichrist, who is characterized by pride, greed, deceit, and who oppresses (and even murders) the poor, helpless, and innocent (the saints of the Lord). For a time he will prosper and his evil deeds will go unchecked (10:3-5), but with the prayers of the humble saints of God (those with prepared hearts, 10:17), God will do justice, so that this wicked man of the earth may oppress no more (Revelation 19:19-20).

Prayer for today: *We praise You, our God, because You know the end from the beginning and are the perfect, just Judge. We rest in the knowledge that both the righteous and the wicked will one day stand before You and receive perfect justice.*

Read Psalms 11-14 *April 21*

Key Verse: Psalm 13:5 *"But I have trusted in Your mercy; my heart shall rejoice in Your salvation."*

In **Psalm 11**, David tells of a time when he found himself in the midst of severe adversity. Some well-meaning friends gave him advice, but he knew better than to listen to them. Their advice was that he take the easy way out and flee to the mountains where he would be safe, since there are many places to hide (11:1b). David, however, chose the way of faith rather than expedience. He knew he should not run from his problems, for that showed a lack of faith in God to see him through. Running away would also displease God, for in such a way David would have failed the test of faith (11:5a). Righteousness and faith are like a foundation, and if it is destroyed, David asks, "What can the righteous do?" He had already given the answer: "In the Lord I put my trust" (11:1a).

Adversity that tests one's faith can be expected in the life of a believer, but God is in control of every situation. It is our job to trust in Him and thus build our faith. God is a watchful King, having all authority and power. He sees all that mankind does, and He is active in the affairs of man. For those who are righteous, He graciously works in their lives to increase their faith, but the wrath of God is the portion for the wicked (11:5-6).

Once again, in **Psalm 12**, David is distressed; this time it is because of the lack of godly men around him and the corruption of his society. He has noticed that the people "speak idly everyone with his neighbor" (12:2), which is unprofitable talk, such as gossip, lying, and flattery. It has been said that flattery is merely treachery in disguise. It is spoken by one with "a double heart" (12:2), namely a hypocrite — one who believes one thing in his heart but speaks another with his mouth. God will not tolerate a person like this, and it is vain for them to think they can get away with such perverse talk (12:3-4). In sharp contrast, we read that "the words of the Lord are pure words"; they have been purified to perfection (seven times), and the believer should meditate upon them (see Phil. 4:8-9). God's Word is the word of truth which will last forever, and no perverse generation, from the time of David until today, has been able to destroy it. The truth of the gospel message has reached to every generation, for God has preserved His Word in the Holy Bible.

Again in **Psalm 13**, the psalmist begins with a distressful situation, but after contemplating God's goodness, he ends on a note of triumph. The historical situation behind this psalm was likely when David was in a long period of exile and hiding as a fugitive from Saul, who sought to kill him. David knew that God had chosen him to be king, but while wearily running and hiding amongst the caves in the wilderness, he began to feel that God had forgotten him. Four times in his prayer he asked God, "how long?" Obviously, David was getting impatient. He prayed, "enlighten my eyes" (13:3), and in this context it is a prayer for added strength to keep on going and not give up, lest his enemy find and kill him. It appears in the ending of the Psalm that God answered his prayer. David did receive new-found strength which came by remembering God's mercy and goodness. When he considered all the ways God had blessed him, he realized that he had no reason to complain, and because he trusted in the Lord, he could be assured of salvation, which in turn put a joyful song in his heart.

The words of the psalmist in **Psalm 14** teach of the universal depravity of man (cf. Eph. 2:1-3; Ps. 51:5). The best example for man's depravity is the fool ("ignorant") who believes there is no God (a practical athiest). Since he believes he will not have to account for his actions, he does whatever he pleases and follows no moral code. He is utterly corrupt and perverse (14:1). Notice how the Bible does not try to prove the existence of God nor does it speculate, for His existence is a reality and the truth.

After surveying the whole world, there would not be one person found whom God could call morally good (14:2; cf. Romans 3:9-12). This has been the case ever since the fall of man. The psalmist longed "that the salvation of Israel would come out of Zion" to bring back the captivity of His people, or in other words bring restoration (14:7). This longing was realized in the coming of Jesus the Messiah. His redemption brings restoration and gladness to the people of God.

Prayer for today: *We magnify Your holy name, oh Lord, as we consider all You've done for us. Your eternal plan of salvation through Jesus has allowed a depraved race to once again have access into Your holy presence and have that fellowship with You for which every human inherently longs.*

Read Psalms 15, 16 &17   April 22

Key Verse: Psalm 17:7b *"O You save those who trust in You."*

The questions David raised in verse one of **Psalm 15** were no doubt prompted by his concern to establish the true worship of God. David wanted to be sure that God would be pleased with the service and worship to Him in the newly erected tabernacle (tent), especially since God had been displeased with the first attempt to bring the Ark up to Jerusalem (2 Samuel 6:1-11). David appointed the Levites for all the various duties in connection with the tabernacle, but he understood that, more than their family lineage, godliness was the key requirement to serve the Lord, dwell near His Holy presence, and approach Him for true worship.

David firstly listed the qualifications of godliness in a positive sense. He saw that godliness must encompass every aspect of one's life: "walks uprightly" having no deviation from the truth (cf. Proverbs 28:18; Isaiah 33:15-17); "works righteousness", putting the truth of God into practice; and "speaks the truth", having pure intentions and honest motivations (15:2). There is no guile or deceit in the true citizen of Zion, for his heart is set on God, and he is thus dependent upon the truth. He does not break the ninth or tenth commandments (does not speak falsely, nor covet) regarding his treatment of a neighbour. He is an honourable man of integrity and one who shows respect, compassion, and kindness to his fellow man (obeys the law — Leviticus 25:35-37; Deuteronomy 16:19; 27:25). All of this stems from the fact that he fears (honours, respects, obeys) the Lord. Those of any nationality, who are born of God by receiving Jesus, are the true citizens of Zion and the royal priesthood of God (John 1:11-13; 1 Peter 2:9-10).

Psalm 16 was likely written during David's days as a fugitive in exile, when he had nothing except the Lord. It beautifully expresses the walk of faith and begins by showing the signs of a believer: one who puts his trust in God, declares Him to be Lord, rejoices to see others living righteously, and has nothing to do with idolatry or those who practice it (16:1-4).

The psalm goes on to express the present blessings of the believer. The greatest blessing is to have the Lord as one's inheritance. In the psalmist's day, the most important possession was land, for they lived off their land. The Levites, however, as wholly consecrated servants of God, were not assigned an allottment of land for their inheritance when they entered the Promised Land, because their inheritance was the Lord (Numbers 18:20). Since the Lord is the believer's inheritance, the believer has the most perfect and pleasant portion; it is like having the best land and nothing more is desired. His cup is full and his thirst has been quenched. In the Lord, the believer finds satisfaction, contentment, and safety (16:5-6). David could confidently say: "I shall not be moved", for he had set the Lord before him, and therefore God, his inheritance, would remain with him (16:8). This brought David great joy, hope, and life (16:9-11).

In this same passage, the Holy Spirit revealed the mystery of the resurrection of Jesus Christ, God's "Holy One", whose body would not see corruption. Such an interpretation was confirmed by the apostles Peter and Paul (Acts 2:25-28; 13:35). It is through Jesus that God shows us "the path of life", for as Jesus Himself said, "Because I live, you will live also" (John 14:19).

Psalm 17 is a desperate prayer of the righteous for vindication, divine intervention, and protection from enemies. It was likely written while David was a fugitive in the wilderness. He was confident of his integrity, since God had tested, visited, and tried him, but nothing evil was found (17:3a). Therefore, he had no doubt that God would save him from the oppression and injustices of his enemies (cf. 1 Samuel 24:11-12).

The reasons David gave for his purity are (1) he had made a strong personal resolution not to transgress the Law of God; it was a deliberate decision of his will, and (2) by the Word of God (reading, meditating, and following it) and through prayer for God's help, he had the strength to keep on the straight and narrow path (17:3b-5). Since he was a faithful and trusting child of God, he was sure that God would hear his prayer and protect him. His only refuge from the threat of the roaring lion (cf. 1 Peter 5:8) was to be found under the all-protective wings of a loving God. So he asked, "Keep me as the apple of Your eye" (17:8), that God might take special care of him as one would care for his pupil, a very precious part of one's body. In this plea, David was asking to be the center of God's attention, so that his life would be delivered from the wicked, worldly men who, unlike himself, had no portion in God. The men of the world receive their satisfaction from their material possessions and children (17:14), but David looks to a fuller satisfaction: "I will be satisfied with seeing your likeness" (N.I.V., 17:15).

Prayer for today: *Thank You, our God, for Your great faithfulness to Your servants. May we learn from David the secret of singing Your praises in the midst of deep despair, for as we do, Your perfect peace and deliverance come.*

Read Psalm 18 April 23

Key Verse: Psalm 18:46 *"The Lord lives! Blessed be my Rock! Let the God of my salvation be exalted."*

In **Psalm 18** David beautifully expresses his love and gratitude to God for delivering him from his "strong enemy", that "violent man" Saul, and others who sought to kill him (vv. 17, 48). David described God as his deliverer and strength, as well as using five figurative terms (rock, fortress, shield, horn, and stronghold, v. 2) to illustrate the greatness of God and the protection He had given him while hiding from Saul. On his own, David would not have had the strength to withstand them. He had to be patient, obedient to God, and persistent in prayer, until the time was ripe for God's miraculous deliverance; but until that came, God was his strength and his protector during hardship and close encounters with death (vv. 4-5).

Finally, when David cried out in distress, God intervened with great power to conquer the enemy. With graphic figures, David described the mighty power, majesty, and fierce wrath of God against the wicked oppressors of His child (vv. 7-15). Yet with His child, He is merciful and gentle; holding him up so that his feet would not slip (vv. 25, 35-36). We learn from David's experience that prayer is definitely the key to seeing God's salvation (cf. Romans 10:13).

David expressed the reason for God hearing his prayer and delivering him: "He delighted in me" (v. 19). Why was God pleased with him? He trusted in the Lord (vv. 2, 30; he had the faith that God would bring deliverance); he was righteous, pure, and blameless; he walked in the ways of the Lord, kept God's judgments and statutes (obeyed God's Word), and kept himself from iniquity (v. 20-24); he was also merciful to others; and therefore God was merciful to him (v. 25). These were the reasons for God's intervention in David's life. If we do these same things, the Lord will also be pleased with us, and He will hear our prayers and bring us "out into a broad place" (v. 19) — a place of safety where there are no snares and no places of ambush set against us, so that no harm can come to us from the enemy, Satan.

Although David had a small army of his own, he did not give any credit to them or to himself for their victory. All the credit was given to God, and if David did display any strength, it was only because God had given it to him (vv. 29, 31-34, 39-50). The victorious deliverance proved God's faithfulness and the truth of His Word. He is indeed "a shield to all who trust in Him" (v. 30). He is indeed the One and only true God who lives and who alone is worthy to be exalted (v. 46). After David's victory, the people would have naturally exalted him as their new king, but David turned that exaltation over to God, his King. David rightly believed that it was a higher honour to be a servant of God than to be a powerful, conquering king.

At the conclusion of the psalm, we find verses of Messianic significance. The Apostle Paul understood David's Lord (v. 49) to be Jesus, who will be praised among the Gentiles of the earth (Romans 15:9) and reign forevermore, bringing the ultimate deliverance from the enemy, Satan.

Prayer for today: *Lord, You are our Solid Rock in an unstable world. Thank You for that firm foundation. Help us to attract others to that stability which they too can experience by placing their trust in You.*

Read Psalms 19 &20 April 24

Key Verse: Psalm 19:1 *"The heavens declare the glory of God...".*

In **Psalm 19**, we read of two great witnesses to the glory of God: the heavens and His Holy Law. Both are sources through which we can come to know God. The first is a universal witness which brings mankind to believe in the existence of God. The second leads one to a deeper and more personal revelation of God.

All over the earth, God's beautiful creation bears witness to His glory. "Day unto day" and "night unto night" reveals knowledge of Himself (19:2). The course of nature continually attests to God's existence and majesty. The bright shining sun God created is considered a great agent in revealing His glory; its intense light and energy is but a token of God's power.

After contemplating God's glory in the heavens, the psalmist turns to consider the glory of God as revealed in His law, testimony, statutes, commandments, and judgments, which are altogether righteous, pure, and enduring forever (19:9). This is not only referring to the Law of Moses (Torah) but the totality of God's revelation through the Holy Spirit-inspired scriptures. The tremendous effects of God's Word upon mankind include: restoring the soul, making wise the simple, rejoicing the heart, and enlightening the understanding (19:7-8). The excellence of God's Word surpasses even the most excellent and desirable things on the face of the earth, such as the purest gold or sweetest honey. The Scripture is the most beneficial thing for mankind. Consider how important it is to read, learn, and practice it! God's Word warns us so we might not see destruction and eternal death, and by faithfully following it, we will be rewarded with God's pleasure upon us.

Knowing the Bible, however, makes mankind aware of his depravity, sinfulness, and guilt, especially when compared to God's righteousness and holiness. David's prayer (19:12-14) is exemplary, and it is echoed in the prayer that Jesus taught us to pray: "And do not lead us into temptation, but deliver us from the evil one" (Matthew 6:13). Mankind needs to continually pray for God's strength and sanctification, for although he can never be sinless, he can strive to be blameless by not allowing sin to have dominion over his life. When one has been redeemed by the Lord and is living victoriously over sin, he can be sure that his prayers will be acceptable in God's sight (19:14).

Psalm 20 is addressed to the king before going into battle and is also a prayer for divine intervention on behalf of the king. It would have been sung as a responsive hymn with the participation of the Levitical choir (20:1-5), the king or high priest (20:6-8), and the congregation (20:9). The petition was for the Lord to go before them into battle and grant them victory. Their battles were fought in the Name of the Lord God of Jacob (20:1, 5), and so when they went out to war, God's name and reputation as a deliverer was at stake. The intent of their prayer, then, was also to invoke God to prove Himself once again to be their Deliverer.

It was their practice to make sacrifical offerings to God before going to war (20:3), and if their offerings were acceptable unto God, then they could be confident that God would be with them to give them victory. Of course, this could not be done as a means to manipulate God, for that is impossible; the outcome was totally dependent upon the will of God (20:4).

There appears to be an interval of time between verses five and six; this was possibly the time for the offering of the sacrifices. Once they were completed, the king or high priest spoke in a prophetic manner to acknowledge that God had accepted the sacrifice and that He would be their saving strength. The speaker knew beyond any doubt that "the Lord saves His anointed" (20:6). Their enemy would put their trust in the most modern of war machines (chariots and horses), but that was in vain, for "they have...fallen". Notice that he declares their defeat as a fact of the past, even though the battle had not yet begun. The Lord's people can put their trust solely in God and be assured of the victory (20:8). Before marching to war, the whole congregation, already confident of the answer, prayed, "Save the king! Answer us when we call!" (N.I.V., 20:9).

Prayer for today: *All of creation shouts forth Your praises, for You, oh Lord, are the great Creator and worthy of all glory. May we be the loudest shouters of all, declaring Your glory to the lost!*

Read Psalms 21 &22   *April 25*

Key Verse: Psalm 22:27a *"All the ends of the world shall remember and turn to the Lord."*

Psalm 21 is closely linked with Psalm 20 and serves as a natural sequel. It is a psalm of thanksgiving to God for answering their prayer for victory over the enemy (Psalm 20). God did fulfill their desire and save the king (20:9), as well as granting him many blessings — all because of the mercy of God and the king's trust in Him (20:3-8). This psalm, like Psalm 22, is clearly Messianic. Only the Lord Jesus can be "blessed forever", and also be blessed with "length of days forever and ever" (21:4, 6). The passage continues to prophetically declare that all those who hate God and have plotted evil against Him and His people will experience His fiery wrath: "the fire shall devour them" (see 2 Thessalonians 1:7-8; Revelation 20:14-15). The congregation of the Lord, however, will forever sing His praises (21:13).

From the first verse of **Psalm 22**, it is clearly evident that this is a Messianic prophecy. It is the most explicit of all psalms that deal with the suffering of the Messiah at the time of His crucifixion (also Psalm 69). Those who do not see this have a veil over their eyes. No doubt some of the experiences within the psalm relate to David personally, but most of them could not possibly have been actual experiences of David (e.g. 22:14-18). The Holy Spirit inspired David to prophetically write these words. The New Testament authors and Jesus Himself understood this psalm as Messianic, and frequently quoted it as being fulfilled in Jesus. Upon the cross, Jesus uttered the exact words of the first question which are so familiar to believers (22:1a; Matthew 27:46). Indeed, when He who knew no sin became sin for us (cf. 2 Corinthians 5:21), God had no choice but to forsake Him and not heed Him; however, God still loved Him, heard Him, and did not forget Him (22:24).

The attitude of the people toward Jesus fulfilled the prophecy: He was "despised of the people" (22:6; Matthew 27:39; Mark 15:29) and put to scorn (Luke 23:35). Even the words of the unbelieving priests and scribes fulfilled this Scripture by applying its words to Jesus: "He trusted in God, let Him rescue Him" (22:8; Matthew 27:43).

We learn of the intimate relationship between the Father and the Son (22:9-10), who had been cast upon God from birth, and who trusted God while yet a nursing child. The anguish caused by the separation from God at the time of the crucifixion, then, was greater than the physical torture, and there was no one to help Him (22:11); all had fled from Him, as the strong and influential priests, pharisees, scribes, and ravenous crowd ("bulls") encircled Him and sought His destruction, "raging and roaring" like their father Satan, the lion, seeking to destroy Him (22:12-13). Then Jesus was handed over to the Romans, and by this time He no longer had any strength and His mouth was parched from thirst (22:14-15; John 19:28). The Romans ("dogs have surrounded Me", 22:16) pierced His hands and feet (22:16) to hang him upon the cross. "They divide My garments among them, and for My clothing they cast lots" (22:18). The fulfilment of this prophecy clearly refers to the conduct of the Roman soldiers, so much so that each of the four gospel writers specifically notes its fulfilment at the crucifixion of Jesus (Matthew 27:35; Mark 15:24; Luke 23:34; John 19:24).

Once the crucifixion and atonement were completed, God answered Jesus' cry for salvation (22:11-21). Jesus was victorious over the evil schemes of Satan (see 21:11), as well as over sin and the grave. The Perfect Sacrifice was acceptable, and His vicarious atonement was effectual and complete, "for He has not despised nor abhorred the affliction of the afflicted; nor has He hidden His face from Him; but when He cried to Him, He heard" (22:24). The risen Lord Jesus now victoriously sings praises to God and He will declare His Name, not only to the Jews (22:22-23) but to the whole world who shall remember the crucifixion, that loving sacifice Jesus made for them, and they shall turn to the Lord (22:27)! The risen Messiah now envisions the results of His suffering: many Gentiles, rich and poor alike, all worshipping God, and all those who were hungry for spiritual sustenance "shall eat and be satisfied" (22:26, 29a). The finished redemptive work of Jesus Christ shall fill them. All will bow down to the Great King of the earth, including those who have died (22:29b; cf. Philippians 2:10-11).

The good news of Jesus' redemption has been preached and experienced throughout every generation. The Lord has always and will always have a posterity to serve Him (22:30) — a faithful remnant who will proclaim the message of what Jesus has done to each successive generation. The good news (gospel) will never grow old and die.

Prayer for today: *Gracious Heavenly Father, thank You for sending Jesus to endure sin's penalty on our behalf and become victorious over death and Satan. May we be Your faithful remnant to proclaim this truth to all generations.*

Read Psalms 23, 24 & 25   *April 26*

Key Verse: Psalm 23:6 *"Surely goodness and mercy shall follow me all the days of my life; and I will dwell in the house of the Lord forever."*

Psalm 23 is probably the best known and widely memorized of all the psalms. It gives peace, comfort, spiritual strength, encouragement, and happiness to all those who trust in the Lord. The analogy of the Shepherd and sheep is found throughout the whole Bible. It points to the kind, compassionate, gentle, and good shepherd, the Lord Jesus Christ. Jesus often referred to Himself as a shepherd, and many New Testament writers and Old Testament prophets spoke of Jesus as the Good Shepherd (John 10:11-19; 26-28; Hebrews 13:20; 1 Peter 2:25; 5:4; Isaiah 40:11; 49:9-10; Jeremiah 31:10-12). He came to seek and to save the lost sheep on whom He had compassion when He saw they were without a worthy shepherd (Luke 15:4-7; Isaiah 53:6). Unlike the selfish shepherds of Israel (Ezekiel 34:2-6), the Lord is the good and faithful Shepherd who lovingly cares, guides, protects, and comforts His sheep. He searches for those that are lost, feeds them, gives them rest, and binds their wounds (Ezekiel 34:11-16). The Lord always held shepherds in high regard, such as the patriarchs, Moses, David, Amos, and the list goes on. David's experience as a shepherd and his lifetime of trusting in God helped him to write this psalm with great insight.

There is a small but significant word; the Lord is called "**My**" shepherd. What gives us the right to consider ourselves His sheep? The preceding psalm provides the basis; it was the atoning sacrifice of Jesus Christ, the Good Shepherd, who gave His life for "the sheep" (Jesus died for the whole world), but those who are **His** sheep are those known by Him (born of the will of God) and those who know Him (John 10:11, 14), because they have "recieved Him", since they "believe in His name" (John 1:12-13).

Consider all the good things enjoyed by the sheep of the Lord: He provides physical sustenance (food and water; 23:1-2) and every temporal need, just as would a typical, gracious and hospitable middle-eastern host (23:5). He gives rest in "green pastures". Such pastures are scarce in the Holy Land, so the shepherd would have to lead the flock from pasture to pasture. The sheep, then, are actively involved in trustfully following the Shepherd, so they might continually find this peaceful rest with Him.

The Good Shepherd, also provides for the spiritual needs of His sheep. By following and obeying Jesus, we are restored to communion with God (23:3). What is the reason the Shepherd leads us in the paths of righteousness? For His Name's sake. It is purely because of His grace, and we have done nothing to deserve it. When we live righteously, it brings honour and glory to the Name of God. The sheep's conduct reflects on the shepherd.

When the sheep travel from one restful pasture to another, they must often pass through narrow valleys with rocky cliffs and caves on either side. The shepherd's guidance and presence provides the sheep with safety from harm (Psalm 78:52-54), so the trustful follower need not fear. The loving shepherd must often use his rod to keep his sheep from wandering into dangerous places where bears or lions may be hiding, and although the rod may hurt sometimes, it is actually a good thing which brings comfort. While in the valley, the "shadow of death" might be seen (23:4), but a shadow does not harm, nor does it lead to death, just as the shadow of a lion does not kill. Wherever there is a shadow, there must also be light. Before the shadow of death, there is the Light of Jesus Christ (27:1; John 8:12), and "He turns the shadow of death into morning" (Amos 5:8). His death abolished death and His resurrection brought the light of life to those who follow Him (2 Timothy 1:10). "Goodness and mercy" not only "follows" but "pursues" the Lord's sheep and they can have the confidence that they will have communion with the Lord forever (23:6).

Psalm 24 is a majestic hymn, likely sung responsively by two choirs — one questioning and the other answering. It was possibly written at the time David successfully and joyously brought the Ark up to Jerusalem (2 Samuel 6:12ff). They sung of God's glory, dominion, and sovereignty over the earth and all His creation (cf. Colosians 1:15-17). They answered that only those who seek Him with a pure heart are worthy to stand before Him. As the procession approached the city of Jerusalem with the Ark, representing the presence of God, they spoke to the gates and doors to open wide to gladly receive their glorious and mighty King.

Psalm 25 is a psalm of the penitant in suplication for God's forgiveness of sin and deliverance from enemy threats. Interestingly, it is an acrostic poem, using the successive letters of the Hebrew alphabet as a framework, and for this reason the thoughts do not flow together as smoothly as in most other psalms. David's trust in the Lord was so great, because he waited in faith on the Lord "all the day". He prayed without ceasing, for he committed all his ways to the Lord. He prayed: "show me", "teach me", and "lead me", so that he would always keep God's covenant, live righteously, and fear the Lord.

Prayer for today: *Dear Lord, thank You for being our Good Shepherd, taking care of our every need. May we continue to follow Your leading, so that we might dwell in Your house forever.*

Read Psalms 26 & 27   April 27

Key Verse: Psalm 27:1 *"The Lord is my light and my salvation; whom shall I fear?"*

It appears that an ungodly and affluent group had come into prominence and were trying to slander King David. In his usual manner, David took the matter to the Lord in prayer, as recorded in **Psalm 26**. David did not claim to be perfect or sinless, for in many other psalms he admitted to guilt and asked forgiveness (e.g. Psalm 25); rather, he plead innocent to the charges laid against him. The "sinister scheme" caused him alarm, and it seems he feared for his life and prayed that God would not allow him to die in the company of bloodthirsty sinners (26:9-10). He cried out to the Lord for vindication, and since he had no hidden sin in his life, he was confident to ask God to "examine", "prove", and "try" his mind and heart (26:2).

David was sure of his integrity, which he proceeds to explain. The integrity for the believer includes: in the positive sense, keeping one's eyes on (meditating upon) the lovingkindness (mercy, grace) of God, and walking in God's truth (obedient to His Word); and in the negative sense, not having fellowship with the wicked, not going into the House of God with hypocrites, and not attending places where evildoers are assembled (26:3-5), for if these wrong things were done, the believer might soon be dragged down with them through their influence.

To be worthy to go before the Most Holy and Righteous God, one must be washed with innocence. The outward sign of the washing of hands symbolizes inner washing and purity (26:6). Inward cleanliness is what the Lord requires of those in His presence (see 24:3,4). David expressed his love for communion with God in His house (the tabernacle), where David would go to praise the Lord with thanksgiving hymns and give Him honour and glory by telling of His "wondrous works" (26:7).

Though others around him had succumbed to temptation and had slipped (such as making and accepting bribes, 26:10), David confidently proclaims, "I shall not slip" (26:1) and strongly asserts, "But as for me, I will walk in my integrity" (26:11). His assurance is based upon his trust in God, for God is merciful and just. Therefore, he asks God to redeem him. He declares with faith that his foot stands "in an even place" on the solid ground of the Word of God; therefore, he will not stumble but will live to again bless the Lord in the congregation.

David's serenity in the Lord, expressed in **Psalm 27**, is also based upon His trust in God. In essence, his words are: "If God is for us, who can be against us?" (Romans 8:31). From experience, David could describe the Lord as his "light", "salvation", and "the strength of [his] life" (27:1; cf. John 8:12; Isaiah 12:2); therefore, David had nothing to fear. It is likely that the circumstances surrounding the writing of this psalm was when Absalom and his army had rebelled against his father, David, and encamped against him for battle (27:3; 2 Samuel 17:26; 18:11-6). They forced David to leave Jerusalem, and while he was encamped at Mahanaim, east of the Jordan, he must have longed to return to Jerusalem, so he could once again go into the House of the Lord to behold His glory and be protected within the Holy Place of His presence (27:4-5). David exhibits total confidence that once again he will be honoured and enabled to go and worship the Lord in His tabernacle at Jerusalem (27:6).

Suddenly, there is a drastic change in David's tone (27:7-14). Possibly time had elapsed and he had become anxious for the Lord's deliverance, although he never doubted God's care for him and still declared complete trust in God. He knew that unlike family members, God would never forsake him, and so he had faith that God would answer his prayers, and he would live to once again receive of His blessings (27:13). The psalmist closed by giving himself some good advice. Until the time of God's deliverance, he resolved not to lose hope nor worry but to be patient and "wait on the Lord" (cf. Isaiah 40:29, 31).

Prayer for today: *In our hour of distress, oh Lord, You hear our cry and are with us. May we not be anxious but wait on You with confidence. When we are trusting in You, whom shall we fear?*

Read Psalms 28, 29 &30 *April 28*

Key Verse: Psalm 29:2 *"Give unto the Lord the glory due to His name; worship the Lord in the beauty of holiness."*

As we learn from **Psalm 28**, David was greatly distressed because he had received no immediate answer to his prayer, yet he knew he could cry out to the Lord, for He was compassionate, kind, and loving. He knew he could depend upon God for deliverance, for He was almighty and just. He felt, however, confused and frightened at the apparent silence of God. It appears that God had delayed His answer to David, just as we may find with our prayers today. But we can be sure that if we are blameless before God and persistent in prayer (keep on knocking), He will answer in His own perfect timing. Surely, the delay is for a purpose, and because of His infinite wisdom we can be sure that all things will work together for good to those who love God (Romans 8:28).

If God, His Rock, did not intervene very soon, David felt he would die. He urgently appealed for God to hear him, for if he had no communion with God, he feared he would suffer the same fate as the wicked: death in the pit (cf. Psalm 88:4). He asked God to protect him from his wicked foes and not include him with them, for he knew God's wrath and retribution awaited them. These people were guilty of hypocrisy (28:3b), forsaking God and denying His power (28:5). David prayed that God would give them their just deserts, according to the measure of their wickedness. Similarily, the Apostle Paul saw wickedness and condemned it (Romans 1:18, 28, 32).

Suddenly, there is a change in tone (28:6). David finally got the victory, causing his outburst of praise and worship! God answered him because David trusted in Him (28:7). David did not lose his faith and confidence in God as His deliverer, even when God seemed so distant. Since David, the king, was strengthened by God, so also were his subjects whom he dearly loved; therefore, he prayed that God would continue to bless and shepherd His people Israel.

The majestic, poetic hymn of **Psalm 29** calls for universal praise and worship to the Lord, since He alone is worthy as the King of all creation, having power over all the forces of nature. The psalmist points to the raging thunderstorm as yet another manifestation of the glory and power of God, which is not only seen but is heard as the powerful and awesome "voice of the Lord" (mentioned seven times). The loud thunder of His voice extends westward over the Mediterranean, northward over the forests of Lebanon, and southward over the wilderness of Kadesh; thus it is echoing and having a great effect over the entirety of the Holy Land, attesting to His majestic presence among His people. It causes everyone to shout, "Glory!", for the Lord God of Israel is the all-powerful King of the world forever. It would have been reassuring for the people of Israel to know that the Almighty, who is able to cause and control the thunderstorms, was on their side to save and protect them. He who can bring great havoc, should He choose, is also the God who can bless His people with great peace, even in the midst of the storm.

Psalm 30 relates the experience of David at a point when he had escaped death, possibly from a serious illness. His miraculous recovery brought great joy to the nation and caused David to exalt the Lord, his healer and deliverer. Now David's foes could no longer rejoice at his suffering or death. This experience caused him to lead the faithful people of Israel in praises to the Lord who had turned their night of weeping into a morning of joy; their mourning into dancing.

After going through the suffering, David had learned that it was God, and God alone, that made his "mountain stand strong" (30:7). His prosperity had caused David to become proud and boast in his self-sufficiency: "I shall not be moved [shaken]" (30:6), but with this, God hid His face from him, and then the troubles came (cf. 1 Peter 5:5-10). His near death situation caused him to realize his total dependency upon God, so that he humbly cried out for mercy, healing, and for God to be his "helper" (30:10). As he pleaded with God to spare his life, David came to understand more fully the purpose of his life on earth: to glorify God and declare His truth to others as a witness for Him. The Apostle Paul also desired to live that he might be a witness for Jesus, but he, having the fuller revelation of God, had a greater understanding of the glorious after-life that awaits the believer (Philippians 2:21-24).

Prayer for today: *Today, Lord, we give You the glory that is due Your Holy Name. You have all authority in heaven and on earth, yet You care so intimately for us as individuals. May our purpose in life be to glorify You and declare Your truth to others.*

Read Psalms 31 &32   *April 29*

Key Verse: Psalm 32:1 *"Blessed is he whose transgression is forgiven, whose sin is covered."*

Once again in **Psalm 31**, David complains about the wicked who are slandering him. The occasion for writing was likely when David was forced to flee because of Absalom's revolt. He was both grieved and humiliated, yet he had confidence in God's deliverance and took refuge in God, whom he expressed as being his Rock and fortress of defense. His total dependence and consecration to God was evident in his words which were made sacred and given a fuller meaning by Jesus' use of them while on the cross: "Into Your hand I commit my spirit" (31:5a; Luke 23:46). At the time, David was not thinking about his death and the final committal of his soul to God, but rather a daily committal of his life and a trust in the Lord for deliverance, based upon his personal experience of God's redemption and truth (31:5b). In every situation of life, especially when near death, the believer must be certain that his spirit is indeed wholly committed to the Lord.

With an intensified appeal to the Lord, David described his grim situation (31:9-18). He knew that God was aware of all his sorrows (31:7) and had already mercifully freed him from the hand of the enemy and brought him to a wide and safe place (31:8 possibly refers to his escape from Absalom by leaving Jerusalem, and the refuge and sustenance God provided in the plains east of the Jordan at the fortified city of Mahanaim, 31:21; 2 Samuel 15:14; 17:24, 27-29).

Though he was "cut off" from praying in the House of God at Jerusalem, David was confident that God still heard his supplications (31:22). As an ousted king, he felt like a "broken vessel" (31:12b) — useless and thrown away. Years of grief over the misconduct of his children and his past sins had taken its toll, and he felt wasted away (31:10); yet he knew God was in control, and his time of deliverance, as well as his time of death, were in God's hands (31:15). By recalling the Lord's past mercies and present help, David was filled with gratitude and faith that God would continue to preserve him (31:23). His trust in God's goodness prompted him to encourage others to also love the Lord and put their hope in Him (31:24).

Psalm 32 brings comfort to the penitent and the assurance of God's forgiveness, restoration, and a renewed joy. The occasion for writing this psalm was most likely after David had experienced the forgiveness of God after repenting of his sin with Bathsheba and the murder of her husband (2 Samuel 11). He had learned from his experience and had important advice to pass on to others. He taught that the truly happy (blessed) person is the one who is forgiven by God.

The three-fold blessing God initiates for the penitent is: (1) forgiveness of transgression (a deliberate trespass in willful rebellion against God and His laws); (2) covering of sin (missing the mark or target, falling short); and, (3) not being charged with iniquity (perversity) but rather being justified, as though no sin had been committed. The blessed result is freedom from the burden of sin and guilt, which David so vividly described. The one whose "sin is covered" has received the atoning work of God by the spilt blood of the Sacrifice upon the Mercy Seat. Jesus shed His blood so that our sins may be covered (Romans 3:24; 1 John 2:2).

Sin is a horrible and frightening thing. It is against God's person, holiness, perfection, and attributes. It is the heaviest burden upon mankind, for it leads to an eternity in hell. While David "kept silent" before confessing his sin and repenting, he was constantly in a state of suffering, both in body and mind, because of his guilt. His conscience would not let him rest, and he felt the wrath of God upon him (32:3-5).

What tremendous relief, cleansing, and comfort David experienced when he confessed his sin openly before God (note 1 John 1:9). Once again, he could say that God was his safe hiding place. Because God's forgiveness is available to all, David also encouraged others to call upon Him while He may be found (cf. Isaiah 55:6; Hebrews 3:13). There will come a day when it will be too late to make a confession of sin. While there is still time, God desires all to come to repentance, that He might have fellowship with them. To further exhort the people to confess their sin before God, David spoke the words of his Great Deliverer who promised to instruct, teach, and guide His children in the way they should go (32:8). David urged them to come to God willingly and submissively, not like a stubborn animal, for fellowship with God brings great joy and inward peace, about which we should sing and shout!

Prayer for today: *Lord God, we confess any sin in our lives which can never be hidden from You. Thank You for Your forgiveness, provided through Jesus, which brings relief from guilt and the comfort of a restored relationship with You.*

Read Psalms 33 & 34   *April 30*

Key Verse: Psalm 34:1 *"I will bless the Lord at all times; His praise shall continually be in my mouth."*

Psalm 33 answers the invitation of Psalm 32:11 (they were originally one psalm), for all the righteous and upright to rejoice in the Lord and shout for joy. The response was one of corporate praise and worship with singing and musical instruments. The ocassion of David's wise and insightful sermon (his testimony of God's forgiveness, Psalm 32) warranted the composition of "a new song" (33:3) of glorification and adoration to God who is to be praised for his goodness and faithfulness, as well as His marvelous creative work of the universe. Alluding to the Genesis account of creation, the psalmist stands in awe and magnifies the Lord who merely had to speak the word, and it was done (33:9).

The Lord's sovereignty is further expressed by contrasting mankind's weak and futile plans with God's enduring and authoritative word, plans, and purposes: "The counsel of the Lord stands forever, the plans of His heart to all generations" (34:11). The greatest plan of God's heart for mankind was the plan of redemption in sending His Son Jesus, so that our souls might be saved from death. Because God loves us, He is truly interested in all we do. His omniscience (all-knowing/all-seeing) is yet another reason the psalmist notes for which He is worthy of praise. For the redeemed, He is the watchful Shepherd and His eye upon them is welcomed (33:18-19); but for the wicked, He is the Judge that punishes, for He not only sees all the deeds of man but understands the heart of man (33:13-15). The song of praise concludes with a prayer of faith: "Let Your mercy, O Lord, be upon us, just as we hope in You" (33:22). In this prayer we are reminded of the words of Jesus when He was called upon to show mercy: "According to your faith let it be to you" (Matthew 9:29).

Psalm 34 is a Hebrew acrostic of praise to God (like Psalm 25) and was written after David's bitter experience of his lack of faith in running from Saul to the Philistine city of Gath and feigning madness before the king, who threw him out. From Gath he escaped to the cave of Adullam where the Lord sent him four hundred men to support him (1 Samuel 21:10-15; 22:1-2). David was humbled and yet enlightened by this experience. Through it, he came to understand more fully the grace and mercy of God, who was his all-sufficiency.

David resolved in his heart to continually praise the Lord, no matter what the situation (34:1; cf. Philippians 4:4; Hebrews 13:15), and like the Apostle Paul, he came to realize that his only boast was in the Lord (Galatians 6:14; Jeremiah 9:23,24). He saw that the Lord was deserving of more than just his own praises, so he urged others to participate with him in worship that would magnify and exalt the Lord.

David's shameful behaviour in Gath was because of fear, but God delivered him from all his fears after he sought the Lord (34:4, likely in the cave of Adullam). David referred to himself as "this poor man", meaning he was desparate, troubled, and in need of help; but with one sincere prayer, God brought him salvation from all his troubles and increased his faith, confidence, and boldness (34:6; cf. 2 Timothy 1:7).

With the familiar words "taste and see that the Lord is good", David challenged the congregation to test God's goodness (cf. 1 Peter 2:3), for if they had but a taste, they would desire more of Him. They would indeed learn that blessed is the man who trusts, fears, and seeks the Lord, for God is faithful to provide for every need (34:8-10; 84:11; Philippians 4:6; Matthew 6:32-34).

David's experiential knowledge gave him the right to warn and instruct others, so that they might not make the same mistakes. He called upon all his children, young and old, to listen to his words of wisdom. By answering his own question, he instructed the people in what they must do to have a long happy life. They were to: 1) keep their tongue from evil and guile, for that which comes from the mouth reflects that which is within the heart; 2) not only depart from evil, but "do good" (put God's law into practice); and 3) not only seek peace but pursue it, which the Apostle Paul teaches as including practicing those things which edify one another (Romans 14:19).

Those who practice righteousness, fear God, and approach Him with humility and brokenness are also blessed with the close presence of the Angel of the Lord, namely our Lord Jesus (34:7, 17-18; Joshua 5:14-15; Isaiah 63:9). From John's gospel, we learn that David was speaking prophetically by referring to Jesus as "the righteous [man]" whose afflictions were many, but God delivered Him, and not one of his bones were broken (34:19-20; John 19:33, 36). Jesus is truly the main character of the whole Bible, not just of the New Testament.

Prayer for today: *Oh God, as we read through the Psalms, our hearts are joined with the psalmist in praise for who You are and all Your wonderful deeds. We too have tasted and have seen that You are good!*

MAY

YEAR TWO
SPRING

A scale model of ancient Jerusalem.
The Temple is on the left.

Special Note: Be sure to write in your request by June 1 for your next volume of *DAY UNTO DAY, the Year Two — Summer* edition. It starts July 1!

Read Psalms 35 &36   May 1

Key Verse: Psalm 36:9 *"For with You is the fountain of life; in Your light we see light."*

In **Psalm 35** the psalmist pictures God as not only a supreme judge but a strong warrior who stands in defense of the helpless (35:1-3, 10; cf. Exodus 15:3; Deuteronomy 32:41). David had felt defenceless before a group of men who were once his friends but were now maliciously slandering him. They had even hired false witnesses to testify against him, just as the strong political/religious party had done to Jesus (Mark 14:57-48). In both cases, it was without just cause or provocation that they rose up against the innocent man, and as the psalmist expressed, "they reward me evil for good" (35:12; John 10:32).

David repeatedly appealed to the Lord to deliver, rescue, and vindicate him from the vicious lions that attacked him and wanted to eat him (35:15-17, 25). He asked that God not only defend him but also pursue his enemies, that they might be brought to justice and be caught in their own nets (35:8). David had faith that God would indeed save his life, preserve his honour, and repay his adversaries with the same dishonour and shame as they had given him. David knew that God had seen all that was done against him (35:17, 22), and according to His righteousness (35:24), He would bring judgment on the wicked. Therefore, with faith he exclaimed that when he was delivered, he would rejoice in the Lord's salvation (35:9), give Him public credit, thanks, and praise (35:18); and he would continually speak of His righteousness and praise (35:28).

In **Psalm 36** the Lord's gracious lovingkindness is beautifully expressed and stands in sharp contrast to the evils of the wicked. In describing his wicked enemy, David points out that his most blatant transgression is in not fearing God. David uses him as a prime example of the wicked who take pleasure in iniquity and hate. Since the wicked man has no fear of God, he ceases doing good and does not reject evil, for he thinks he is not accountable to anyone (36:3-4). He is the total opposite to the one David had previously described in Psalm 34 as the type of person who does fear God and who is blessed with a long happy life (34:11-14).

With beautiful words of adoration to the Lord, the psalmist likens several attributes of God to the different wonders of nature. He describes the mercy, faithfulness, righteousness, and judgments of the Lord which are so great and awesome that they are incomprehensible to the finite mind of man. He concludes that the God who is so great is truly the preserver of both man and beast. In Him all things have their being. He sustains all of His creation.

The attributes of God most precious to man is His loving kindness (36:7). The Hebrew word *hesed*, translated as loving kindness, is pregnant with meaning. It is a steadfast love which is based upon the grace and mercy of God, and because of it, David thanked the Lord, saying: "Therefore the children of men put their trust under the shadow of Your wings" (36:7). As well as providing protection for those who trust in Him, the Lord has given general grace to all mankind by providing them with food and water from His plentiful earth (36:8). Those who seek Him, however, find that within Him is the fountain of life (36:9), not only because he is the ultimate source of all natural life, but because He provides the water of life through Jesus Christ who came to give true life and life ever-lasting (cf. John 4:10, 14) — a spiritual life wherein we have been called out of darkness into His marvelous light (1 Peter 2:9) so we might enjoy life to its fullest. It is in Jesus, the Light of the world, that mankind receives the light of life (cf. John 1:4-5, 9; 1 John 1:5-7; 2 Corinthians 4:6).

Prayer for today: Heavenly Father, thank You for the Light of the world, our Lord and Saviour Jesus Christ, who came that we might have life, and have it more abundantly. May Your light shine through us today to a darkened world.

Read Psalm 37   *May 2*

Key Verse: Psalm 37:4 *"Delight yourself also in the Lord, and he shall give you the desires of your heart."*

Psalm 37 was written in an alphabetic acrostic style, and many of the thoughts are in the form of proverbs. David wrote it toward the end of his life. His experience with the Lord had taught him much and given him much wisdom to share. The psalmist may have been disturbed by an erroneous point of view regarding the justice of God who allowed the wicked to flourish and the righteous to suffer. David's purpose in writing this psalm was to counsel and teach the correct understanding of the prosperity and success of the wicked (cf. Job 20:5; Psalm 49 and 73) by addressing the issue of the inheritance of the righteous (vv. 9, 11, 18, 22, 29, 34).

When the godly people understand that it is not a material issue, but a spiritual one that is of utmost importance, then there is no reason for them to be envious, concerned, or angry about the success of the wicked (v. 1, 8; cf. James 1:9-12; 2 Corinthians 4:17-18). The poor righteous people are in a much better position than the wealthy wicked (v. 16); so rather than being jealous, the godly should occupy their time with putting into practice their faith and trust in God by doing good. David instructs them to feed on the Good Shepherd's faithfulness (v. 3), meaning to rely on Him for their every need, since in all David's years he had "not seen the righteous forsaken, nor his descendants begging bread" (v. 25).

David also advised that God's people "delight" themselves in the Lord (v. 4a). This means to take pleasure in Him by getting to know Him better, reading and meditating upon His Word, having communion (fellowship in prayer) with Him, loving Him, following Him, and doing His will. If these things are done, the believer will have a very close relationship with God; his steps will be ordered by God (v. 23); his spirit will be in tune with God; his life will be in harmony with the Lord's ways; he will abide in God and God's words will abide in him, and whatever he asks of the Lord will be given to him (John 15:7), for the desires of his heart will be the desires of God (v. 4b). They will not be selfish requests but requests that will bring glory to God (cf. James 4:2-3)

David further advises the godly to continue to trust in God and commit their ways to Him, then one day the Lord shall publically honour them for their righteousness (v. 5-6). Believers in Jesus know that He is the way (John 14:6), and the only true righteousness is that which comes through faith in Him (Philippians 3:8-9). Jesus is the Light and the One who can give real inner peace, and He dispells all anxiety about the concerns of this world and the seeming triumph of the wicked (cf. Micah 7:8-9). The psalmist urges the righteous to "wait patiently for Him" (v. 7a), for He has all things in control, and the time of judgment and vindication will surely come (James 5:7-9). The evildoers will be cut off, for the Lord is just (v. 28), and the righteous who have patiently waited will not only be vindicated but (the meek) shall inherit the earth and enjoy "the abundance of peace" (v. 11), which is far better than the temporary material abundance of this life (Matthew 5:5; Isaiah 29:19-20).

What is the main lesson of this psalm? It is to rest in the Lord, for He knows the glorious destiny of His people and laughs at the futility of the wicked (v.13; Proverbs 1:31, 33). God will not forsake the righteous. Therefore rest confidently, knowing God is in control (Hebrews 13:5; Romans 8:18).

Prayer for today: *Dear Lord, help us to keep an eternal perspective so we might not be overwhelmed by the temporal concerns of life. The desire of our heart is to yield to Your desires.*

Psalm 38:18 *"For I will declare my iniquity; I will be in anguish over my sin."*

Psalm 38 is one of brokenness and anguish before the Lord as a result of sin. It is yet another psalm of penitence (like Psalm 6, 25, 32, 51, 102, 130 and 143). David repented of his sin, but still the sorrow of the sin remained in his memory, so this psalm is entitled "remembrance". It may also relate to one of the Levitical offerings of incense unto the Lord, wherein God's forgiveness is remembered in answer to prayer and the offering of atonement. God, however, had forgiven David, and once God forgives, the sin is not remembered but forgotten (Isaiah 43:25; 44:22).

David knew he had sinned and that a divine rebuke was necessary; so as he began to pray, he did not ask God to withhold His rebuke or chastisement, but he asked that His wrath be removed from those punishments (38:1). The believer cannot bear divine wrath, but divine chastisement, which is done in love, is beneficial and should be welcomed, for it leads us to partake more in God's holiness, and because of it we know God loves us and that we are His children (Proverbs 3:11; Hebrews 12:5-11). Once David confessed his sin and repented, the wrath of God would no longer be upon him.

The particular sins for which David repented were likely his adultery with Bathsheba and the murder of her husband, for this was the most grievous point of his life (2 Samuel 11; 12:13-14). David referred to his sin as "iniquity" (38:4, 18), which is a perversity that implies a moral failure. His unconfessed sin was like an unbearable, heavy load upon him (38:4), and it turned to mental and spiritual anguish (depression, fear, and anxiety), which then gave rise to physical infirmities. David felt as though arrows from God were piercing him (38:2). Truly the Holy Spirit was putting him under the conviction of his sin, and he was racked with guilt (38:8).

Like Job, his friends and family abandoned him as though he had a contagious disease like leprosy, and his enemies saw it as an opportune time to lash out at him. Throughout the persecution, David reacted in the same manner as did Jesus when He was accused; he remained silent (38:13-14; Matthew 27:12-14). He knew God was still watching him (38:9) and was confident that God would vindicate him and bring justice to the wicked. David did not have to defend himself; God would defend His own honour and the honour of His representative. David showed true repentance by being sincerely sorry for the sin itself, not merely for the results the sin brought. He closed his petition for mercy with a confident prayer, believing that his compassionate God would quickly bring salvation.

Psalm 39 appears to be a sequel to the previous psalm, but here David seems in even deeper despair. He feels his life will soon be over but still has hope, and therefore he is awaiting the Lord's deliverance. Psalm 38 spoke of his silence before men, but here the psalmist has resolved to be silent before God and man, lest he complain against God, as did Job. From the similarities, it appears the psalmist was familiar with the Book of Job, and he learned from Job the folly of trying to contend with God. Since the wicked people were around him, possibly tempting him to curse God, the psalmist did not want to criticize God's ways, lest they hear and he do harm to the cause of the righteous.

His bitterness within, however, was smoldering, and he had to give vent to his feelings. Finally, when he spoke to the Lord, he wanted to know how much longer he must suffer from His plague before death would overtake him. He felt wasted away and very insignificant. He also felt that compared to God, who is without age, he is but a vapour and the work he does and the wealth he heaps up during his lifetime is all in vain (39:5-6; cf. Ecclesiastes 1:18; 5:16). In the natural, he is without hope, but it is only with God that he has any hope, for without God life is truly futile.

The psalmist is repentant, for he realizes that it is only after the Lord has delivered him from all his transgressions (39:8a) that there will be real purpose to his life. With his new-found hope, he has the faith to ask and believe that God will hear him, heal him, and look upon him with lovingkindness rather than wrath, so that his strength may be renewed.

Prayer for today: *We praise You, Oh God, for Your forgiveness that removes our sin as far as the east is from the west. We pray that nothing in our lives would hinder our treasured relationship with You, that we might draw even closer.*

Read Psalms 40&41 May 4

Key Verse: Psalm 40:1 *"I waited patiently for the Lord; and He inclined to me, and heard my cry."*

What wonderful rewards the believer receives when he waits patiently for the Lord by persevering in prayer, trusting that His will be done in His own perfect timing and resting secure upon His Word. In **Psalm 40** we learn that the Lord graciously answers those who wait upon Him (cf. Psalm 27:14; Isaiah 40:31). He lifts them up as His own precious children and puts them on sure ground, so they might not fall again and get hurt (40:1-2). He gives them a new song of praise to the Lord, for in their experience of chastening they had learned to be more conformed to the holiness of God and the image of Jesus Christ. It is a wonderful witness to others of the grace and goodness of God when he lifts up, restores, and gives new and better understanding to His children; this causes others to put their trust in the Lord (40:3).

Those who do trust the Lord are called blessed. They do not have to lie, deceive, and side with the rich and proud in order to be sure all their needs will be met, for the Lord is the source of all blessings, and He takes loving care of His children. With these thoughts of God's goodness in mind, the psalmist begins to praise Him for the abundant kindness and wonderful deeds that He has done for those who trust in Him. On the basis of His lovingkindness, the psalmist can plead with faith for the Lord to preserve and deliver him (40:11, 13, 17).

In the middle of the psalmist's words of praise, it appears that the Spirit of prophecy came upon him (40:6-10). He declares that the Lord had opened his ears to hear and have better understanding. He learned that sacrifices and offerings are not adequate to express gratitude to God, for He desires sincere praises that come from a pure heart. Nor does the sacrificial blood of bulls and goats make adequate atonement for sin. Only the blood of the Most Perfect Sacrifice, Jesus Christ, could accomplish that (Hebrews 9:12-14). Read what the writer of the Epistle to the Hebrews penned referring to Jesus in Hebrews 10:5-10). Who better than Jesus could say that it was written of Him in the Book? Who more than Jesus delighted to do God's will? Who more than Jesus openly declared the good news of righteousness, God's faithfulness, salvation, lovingkindness, and truth? He Himself was the embodiment of these very things. We, His servants, are to be like Him and do the same. We must delight to do God's will, and one way this is accomplished is by keeping God's Word within our hearts.

Psalm 41 begins with a beatitude that is similar to the words of Jesus: "Blessed are the merciful, for they shall obtain mercy" (Matthew 5:7). The psalmist David seems to be referring to himself as the one who had shown mercy and helped the poor; so on this basis, he has the faith that God will also help him in his time of need, deliver him from his enemies, preserve his life, comfort and strengthen him on his sickbed. Therefore, he called upon the Lord, yet he recognized that for God to answer him, it was not merely enough for him to be doing good to others; he understood that his spiritual life must be right with God, so he humbly confessed his sin (41:4).

The occasion for the composition of Psalm 41 appears to be when Absalom and his co-conspirators were scheming against David and spreading malicious rumours in order to turn the people against him and support Absalom (2 Samuel 15:3-6). History tells us that their smear campaign was quite effective. Even David's friend and personal advisor, Ahithophel, turned against him (41:9; 2 Samuel 15:12, 31).

David was content, however, to leave the retribution up to the Lord (e.g. 2 Samuel 16:11-12). He did not desire private revenge, but once the Lord had raised him back to the throne, he desired to call them to account for their treason against him as the Lord's chosen king. If and when the Lord would return him to a place of honour, then David would be confident that God was pleased with him as His choice for king.

Prayer for today: *Thank You, Lord, that You do hear our cry. May we be patient in prayer and wait for Your perfect answer in Your perfect time.*

Read Psalms 42, 43&44   *May 5*

Key Verse: Psalm 43:3 *"Oh, send out Your light and Your truth! Let them lead me; let them bring me to Your holy hill and to Your tabernacle."*

Psalms 42 and 43 were originally one compostion. The beautiful poetic style is the same in both, as is the subject matter. It appears from the title that the poem was written by a leading member of the Levitical musical guild (43:4) from the Kohathite division of the sons of Korah (1 Chronicles 6:31-37). No doubt the psalmist was a captive of an ungodly nation (42:9b; 43:1) and may have been en route to a foreign country when he penned these words.

He finds himself far from Jerusalem, northeast by the headwaters of the Jordan on the slopes of Mount Hermon (42:6), along the caravan route between Syria and the far east. His strongest desire is to commune with God. He needs this as much as he needs water to live, for God is his fountain — his source of life (cf. Jer. 2:13; Psalm 63:1; 84:2; John 4:14; 6:35). He longs to go once again to Jerusalem and worship the Lord "with the voice of joy and praise" (42:4b); but since he could not, he was extremely sorrowful. As he sees and hears the rapids of the Jordan, he feels waves of grief coming over him (42:7).

His enemies constantly taunt him regarding the seeming indifference of his God: "Where is your God?" (42:3b, 10b). Surely he retorted that His God would deliver him, but questions flooded his mind and he was greatly distressed. Had God forgotten him and cast him off? (42:9; 43:2). In his heart he knew that God was still watching over him and that God would still give him a song to sing (42:8). With faith he declared that there was still hope and he would one day lift his voice in praise to God again in the tabernacle on His holy hill (42:5, 11; 43:5). He turns from despair to hope, from doubt to assurance, and from confusion to a resolution of strong faith. He prayed that God's light and truth would lead him back to the Lord's presence (43:3). The Light and truth of God have been personified in Jesus Christ, and He is the One to lead us into the presence of God (John 1:4-5, 9, 17).

Psalm 44 is another psalm ascribed to the sons of Korah. The psalmist writes of a disturbing military defeat and a captivity of his people. The historical occasion this psalm addresses is unknown. The psalmist complains bitterly to the Lord that there was no justification for Him to allow such a thing to happen. He claims that Israel/Judah had remained faithful in following the Lord, and so the psalmist is confused and upset that God allowed such a calamity to overtake them. In the past, God had always fought for them and saved them (44:4-7). If they had turned to idolatry, then the psalmist says such a thing would be understandable and even expected, but they did not; they were faithful to the Lord. Why then had this terrible calamity come upon them?

The psalmist, like any other person, could not understand the ways of God, but we know that the Lord has a purpose in whatever He allows to happen to His children, and it is for their ultimate good, although to them it may not seem so at the time. The situation described is in effect asking, "Why do the righteous suffer?" At that time, they did not have the fuller revelation of God which teaches us that it is not unusual for the godly to suffer (Matt. 5:11; John15:20, 25; Acts 14:22; Rom. 8:36; 2 Tim. 3:12). Trials are a means God uses to refine His people. Their suffering and exile would sift them like wheat. Those who are truly committed to the Lord will remain faithful to Him, and those who are not will be caught up in the idolatry of the surrounding nations and be blown away like chaff in the wind. Thereby, God is reserving a faithful remnant for Himself.

The psalmist was in turmoil and confusion about the whole situation, but he still had the faith and sense to call upon God, for truly the Lord is merciful and hears the prayers of His people.

Prayer for today: *Heavenly Father, our desire is to worship You and daily grow closer to You, even though this growth may require trials and testings. With joy we will endure, knowing we are part of Your faithful remnant (James 1:2-4).*

Read Psalms 45, 46&47   *May 6*

Key Verse: Psalm 47:8 *"God reigns over the nations; God sits on His holy throne."*

When **Psalm 45** is studied with the spiritual eye, one can clearly see that it is a Messianic Psalm. It paints a beautiful picture of Jesus Christ, the royal and majestic Bridegroom coming for His well-prepared bride, the Church (Revelation 19:7). In the immediate context, however, the psalm was a wedding hymn which was likely sung at royal weddings. It is difficult to ascertain for which earthly king it was originally composed.

The psalmist declares that his tongue was as the pen of a "ready writer" (45:1b). He was prepared in his spirit as a prophet to utter and to write as the Holy Spirit inspired. With these beautiful words of praise to the King, we can envision the majesty of His coming for His bride. He is more beautiful than any mortal. The Bridegroom's words reflect the divine grace within His heart (45:2). Who but our Lord Jesus is full of grace, "truth, humility, and righteousness" (45:4). He will "ride prosperously" as a conquerer when He comes for His bride (45:3-5; Revelation 6:2). Who but our Lord Jesus carries a scepter of righteousness and has a throne that will last forever and ever (45:6). These very words (45:6-7) were applied to Jesus Christ by the writer of the Epistle to the Hebrews (Hebrews 1:8-9).

All believers are children of the King. The Bride is the King's daughter, and she is being counselled that marriage to the Bridgroom entails the separation from everything familiar to her so she might cling only to her husband (45:10-11). At the rapture, all the saints of God will leave everything behind to go and live with the Groom, our King Jesus. There will be no regrets; it will be the happiest occasion for the bride, who is described as "glorious within", for she will be pure and undefiled (2 Corinthians 11:2; Ephesians 5:27). She will enter the King's awesome palace which will be her new home. The Bridegroom is now preparing the place for His bride, and one day it will be the site of the joyous Marriage Supper of the Lamb, where the bride will worship Him (45:11, 14-15; John 14:1-3; Revelation 19:7-10).

Psalm 46 is a beautiful poem that sings out the praises of God and gives assurance that He is our refuge and help. The historical situation of this psalm may have been when the mighty forces of Sennacherib encamped against Jerusalem, during the days of Hezekiah, and God miraculously delivered them by sending His angel to smite 185,000 in one night (2 Kings 19:20-37), thus putting an end to the war (46:8-9).

The psalm gives a wonderful example of peace in the midst of turmoil. Whatever the storm may be on the outside, we can have confidence that inside the refuge of the Lord there will be calm and rest, and those inside need not fear. These storms build character in the believer, as well as spiritual strength, increasing his faith and making him steadfast upon the "Rock of Ages" that will not be shaken. Jerusalem was not shaken because the Lord of Hosts (over His angelic army), the God of Jacob (the faithful God of the covenant), was with them ("Emmanuel", Matthew 1:23; Romans 8:31). Although there is no river in Jerusalem, God sustained and gave joy to His people with the river of His grace (46:4-5; Isaiah 58:11). With His all-powerful voice, the Lord of Hosts uttered His will, "the earth melted" and the war was over (46:6; cf. Hebrews 12:26). He will do the same in the apocalyptic battle when the Prince of Peace will end all wars on earth and bring universal peace. At that time, all will know that He is God and He will be exalted in all the earth.

Psalm 47 is a continuation of the previous psalm, and it too has a prophetic aspect. It is a celebration song to the exalted King, our Lord Jesus, who will reign and rule over all the earth. After the Lord won the battle for His people (Psalm 46), He ascended back to His great throne. The psalmist now calls Him the Lord Most High who is worthy of universal praise, for He is the great King over the whole earth (cf. Jeremiah 10:6-7; 1 Timothy 1:17; 6:15-16). He will subdue all peoples (2 Corinthians 15:24-28). His great deeds demand shouts of triumph and claps of joy. His transcendence and majesty demand endless songs of praise. All believers in Jesus, the people of the God of Abraham, will gather together to worship and exalt His Holy Name (cf. Romans 4:16-17; Galatians 3:7, 14, 29). To them whom He loves, the Lord will give an incorruptible and undefiled inheritance (47:4; 1 Peter 1:4). What a wonderful hope we have in the King of Kings and Lord of Lords!

Prayer for today: *Dear Lord, our hearts are filled with joyful anticipation as we read these prophetic psalms. Oh that we, Your bride, will be prepared for Your coming and continue to reach others until that glorious day!*

Read Psalms 48, 49&50 May 7

Key Verse: Psalm 50:23 *"Whoever offers praise glorifies Me; and to him who orders his conduct aright I will show the salvation of God."*

Psalm 48 is related to the previous two psalms, forming a trilogy of praise which is also seen as being apocalyptic in nature, yet it does have an historical basis. This psalm describes the greatness of God and the glory of His city Jerusalem, which He preserved in a miraculous way. Since He was the King of the world (Psalm 47:7), the city where He chose to put His Name and the site of His Holy Temple deserves honour. He protected Jerusalem from the combined forces of several kingdoms when they came to lay seige against the city (likely referring to the events during the reign of Jehoshaphat, 2 Chronicles 20:1-9, 22-24, 27-30). The enemies' plans against the city were destroyed just as easily as when God sent the east wind to destroy "the ships of Tarshish" (a particular type of ship, but not necessarily from Tarshish, south of Spain;1 Kings 22:48; Ezekiel 27:25).

The people of Jerusalem had heard that the Lord of Hosts would protect His city, but now they saw with their own eyes that it was indeed true. Jerusalem's refuge was in God (48:3b, 8; 2 Chronicles 20:14-20). Since it was clear that God had laid claim to Jerusalem, they beleived that God would establish it forever as His eternal city (the earthy city will pass away, but the New Jerusalem will remain forever, Hebrews 11:10, 16; 12:22; Revelation 21:2). The psalm began with the exhortation that the Lord be praised "in the city of our God", but after considering His lovingkindness, the worshippers proclaim that He deserves to be praised "to the ends of the earth" (48:9-10). By looking at the sacred places in Jerusalem, the worshippers are reminded of God's goodness and lovingkindness to them and that He would always be their guide, because He was in their midst.

Psalm 49 is directed to all people from all classes, since the message of the Lord is for everyone, and it is the task of His chosen people to proclaim it. The psalmist says that he will reveal some wise words for the purpose of meditating upon the mystery of life (49:4). Since he trusts in the Lord, he has nothing to fear (49:5), but he warns that those who trust in their wealth do have something to fear. No amount of money can ever be used as a ransom for the soul; it cannot rescue anyone from death and decay in the grave (cf. Mark 10:24). The redemption of the soul is costly — something money cannot buy (49:7-9). Only God Himself can redeem a person's soul from the power of the grave (49:15). Our loving God who condescended to become a man, Jesus Christ, paid the price by sacrificing His life to redeem our souls from eternal death (the punishment of sin), that by His shed blood we might have everlasting life (Hebrews 9:12-15; 2 Timothy 1:10; 1 Corinthians 15:20-26, 55; John 5:24).

To encourage the upright who struggle with the age-old question of the prosperity of the wicked (49:16), the psalmist reminds them that wealth cannot be taken with anyone when they die, nor can it buy the wicked salvation: "They shall never see light" (49:19) — the light of life that Jesus gives to those who are His own. All mankind will die and be judged (Hebrews 9:27), yet for the upright there is hope. They "shall have dominion over them [the wicked] in the morning", on that grand and glorious resurrection morning, they shall see the Light when Jesus Christ comes and gives them eternal life with Him (John 5:24-29; 1 John 5:12; 1 Thessalonians 4:14-16).

In **Psalm 50**, the Lord comes with a manifestation of His glory as the righteous Judge over His covenant people (Exodus 24:3-8). He summons them together, for they are in need of rebuke. They offer him many sacrifices, but the problem is that they have not properly worshiped Him from their heart, and God is interested in the condition of the heart and the motivation behind the sacrifice. All the animals of sacrifice belong to Him, so how can they give Him anything? For the sake of atonement, however, the animals were required. What God desired from His people, as He still does today, was their sincere offering of thanksgiving and their obedience to the covenant stipulations. God wants to see that His people have first offered themselves to Him in total submission and absolute loyalty (50:14; for further study on this topic see Mal. 1:7-8; Isa. 1:11-17; Jer. 7:21-23; Michah 6:6-8; Rom. 6:13; 12:1-2; 1 Cor. 6:20; John 4:23; Heb. 13:15-16). In doing this, the faithful people bring glory to God, and God will be faithful to them and deliver them in times of trouble.

The Lord then addresses those Israelites that know the Law, and even teach it to others, while they themselves do not practice it. They are compromising and hypocritical, and the sin of hypocrisy is detestable to God. For a while the Lord was silent about their behaviour, but He promises to call them to account. He warns them to change their wicked ways, lest they perish and not find salvation. Those who glorify God through praise from a pure heart and live righteously by following His ways will indeed see the salvation of God (50:23).

Prayer for today: *Lord, You are great, and greatly to be praised. May our worship not be merely out of duty or formality but from a sincere motivation of our heart. And may our conduct be worthy of Your salvation as it reflects that which is in our heart.*

Read Psalms 51, 52&53   *May 8*

Key Verse: Psalm 51:10 *"Create in me a clean heart, O God, and renew a steadfast spirit within me."*

Psalm 51 is the most profound of all the psalms of penitence by King David. In it we see his deepest emotional confession and plea for forgiveness. Down and through the years, it has been the model prayer for the penitent. The occasion for David's writing of this psalm would have been shortly after his commiting adultery with Bathsheba and murdering her husband Uriah (for further information see commentary on 2 Samuel 11 & 12). His sin (adultery, deception, lies, conspiracy, and murder) is so great that all he can do is fall on the mercy of God. He envisions his transgression as being recorded in God's register, and so he asks that it be blotted out, that God may forgive him and remember it no more (51:1, 9; cf. Isaiah 43:25).

He is deeply convicted of sin and feels the need to be cleansed from the ever-present filthiness of sin in his life (51:2-3, 7; Isaiah 1:18). He alludes to the religious ritual of cleansing through the use of a hyssop branch to sprinkle the blood of the sacrifice upon that which was defiled, that it (or a person) may be purged and sanctified to the Lord's service (Hebrews 9:14,19; Numbers 19:18; Leviticus 14:4-6). David can do nothing to make himself pure; it is the work of God upon his heart, so he pleads with God to create in him a clean heart (Ezekiel 11:19-20; 36:25-26) and to give him a steadfast spirit, that he might not fall into temptation again (51:10).

Once God forgave, cleansed, and delivered David from blood-guiltiness (for the murders of Uriah and those who fell with him, 2 Samuel 11:17), then the joy of God's salvation and fellowship could be restored. David promises that if God would restore and uphold him, he will use his strength to lead other sinners to the Lord, and he will once again sing praises to God (51:12-15).

He is aware that his sin is more than just a sin against man; it is a sin against God, who is holy, pure, just, and blameless. David, however, is the total opposite: born in iniquity and conceived in sin (51:5). He is not saying that his mother sinned at the time of his conception or that he was conceived out of wedlock, but his intent is to express the general sinful condition of all people as natural-born sinners since the Fall of Adam (total depravity of man/original sin). This is not a basis for an excuse, for David makes no excuses. He knew that he was guilty and that he, like Saul, deserved to be cast away from God's presence. He was horrified at the thought of being denied the presence of the Holy Spirit, for he had seen the result of this in the misery of Saul (1 Samuel 15:26; 16:14). Unlike Saul, however, David was truly humble and sincerely repentant; this is what made him a man after God's own heart. No, God would not cast David out. The Lord accepted the sacrifices of his broken spirit and contrite heart (51:17). King David encouraged his subjects to sacrifice unto the Lord, but he understood that if the worshipper's heart and motivation was not right, then God took no pleasure in their sacrifices; they must be "sacrifices of righteousness" or else they are futile, for God sees the heart (51:19; Isaiah 1:11-17; Amos 5:21-22; Romans 12:1-2; Hebrews 13:15).

We learn from the title of **Psalm 52** that it was written against the wicked tyrant Doeg the Edomite who deceived and betrayed David (1 Samuel 21:1-9; 22:9-10). The worst crime of Doeg was that he spoke lies to Saul in order to bring destruction, gain Saul's favour, and thus be rewarded with riches and position; therefore, David condemns and curses him because he "strengthened himself in his wickedness" (52:7b). David was utterly disgusted with such a person who took pleasure in doing evil. Doeg was violent and unscrupulous. He was not only the cause but also the hatchet man of the great and terrible massacre of the priests and their families at Nob (1 Samuel 22:11-22). David prophesies that just as he had invaded homes and destroyed lives, so God would destroy him and pluck him out of his dwelling place. He would then be held up to ridicule and mockery by the righteous. Because Doeg was a traitor, who trusted in his riches and his own strength and not in God, God would uproot him from the land of the living. In sharp contrast, David, who trusted in the mercy of God, was like a firmly planted green olive tree (which has a very long life, representing peace, blessings, fruitfulness, and patriotism).

Psalm 53 is very similar to Psalm 14, except that it has been adapted or revised by the same author for use under a different, yet similar, set of circumstances. The psalmist expresses the total depravity and corruption of mankind in an even stronger way (compare 14:1b; 53:1b), and exposes the ignorance and foolishness of the practical athiest who denies the presence and power of God. Verse five is totally revised (compare with 14:5-6) to suit the new situation. It speaks of the enemy having fear where there was no visible reason to fear. It may refer to the defeat of the Ammonite coalition in the days of Jehoshaphat (2 Chronicles 20:22-24), or possibly the fear of the Syrian army caused by the supernatural force (2 Kings 7:6-7). When the ultimate salvation of the Lord comes, namely the Messiah Jesus who set the captives free, then the Lord's people will have even more reason to rejoice (53:6), but the fool who says, "There is no God" will be in great sorrow and will be no longer able to deceive himself.

Prayer for today: Dear God, with the sincerity of David, we humbly repent of any sins and ask that You create within us a clean heart. Thank You for the blood of Jesus which cleanses from all unrighteousness.

Read Psalms 54, 55&56   May 9

Key Verse: Psalm 55:22 *"Cast your burden on the Lord, and He shall sustain you; He shall never permit the righteous to be moved."*

From the title of **Psalm 54**, we learn that David wrote it when the Ziphites betrayed his whereabouts to Saul (1 Samuel 23:15, 19-29). Although the Ziphites were a clan within the tribe of Judah (David's tribe), they were ungodly, and thus David referred to them as "strangers" who rose up against him. The "oppressors" were Saul and his men, who were seeking to kill David (54:3; 1 Samuel 23:15). Both groups of adversaries had not set God before them; so David describes their actions as an evil for which God would bring retribution (54:3b, 5).

With assurance of deliverance from his divine helper, David declared that God would uphold his life; this gave him peace and rest in the midst of trouble (54:4; Isaiah 41:10; John 14:16-18). His great faith permitted him to speak as though the future deliverance of God had already been accomplished, and he vowed to offer unto the Lord the sacrifice of thanksgiving and praise (cf. Psalm 50:14, 23; Hebrews 13:15).

As the historical records show, the Lord was indeed faithful to deliver David from the evil plans of Saul and the Ziphites. Just at the time when David's capture and death seemed inevitable, the Lord intervened by raising up the Philistines to attack the country, thus causing Saul to leave his pursuit of David to fight the other battle (1 Samuel 23:26-29).

David's faith and dependence upon God's help endured, even after he became king, as is evident in **Psalm 55**. The occasion for writing was most likely when he was confronted with the rebellion of Absalom (2 Samuel 15:7-13). The treachery against David by his own son affected him so deeply with emotional hurt that he groaned and felt physical pain (55:2, 4). He wished he could flee like a bird to a safe place of refuge in the Lord and be far from his enemies and the dangers all around him, for they were busy night and day in his city spreading lies and strife. What made it worse was that among those who turned against him was his close friend with whom he had a covenant and with whom he worshipped God (55:12-14, 20-21). This is likely a referring to Ahithophel, David's former companion and private advisor (2 Samuel 15:12). David came to understand that Ahithophel was a hypocrite who spoke words full of deception and guile. David prayed for God to "divide their tongues" (55:9) which is reminiscent of God's judgment upon the people of Babel in bringing confusion, division, and a stop to their evil plan. God answered this prayer through Hushai, David's true friend, who infiltrated Absalom's inner circle as a spy and foiled Ahithophel's plans against David (2 Samuel 15:34-37; 17:7).

David found that place of refuge through constant prayer, (55:17) casting his burden on the Lord who sustains him. When troubles give us a heavy heart, the wisest action is to unburden ourselves upon the Lord, for He truly cares for us and will sustain us through any circumstance. David prayed that God would bring quick retribution and that his enemies would perish in their prime (55:15, 23). He was confident that the Lord would answer this prayer, because he had faith that God would redeem him and that He punishes those who do not fear Him (55:19; cf. 2 Samuel 17:23; 18:7).

In **Psalm 56**, David once again laments over his treatment by his enemies, and this time it is the Philistines who he asks God to punish in His wrath (56:7). The occasion for the psalm given in the title was when David was captured by the Philistines in Gath. There were two occasions when David went to Gath, but it is most likely referring to the first time when he fled there from Saul, was captured, feigned insanity, and was thrown out by the king (1 Samuel 21:10-21:1); the second time, he and his small army went there voluntarily, yet because he was in exile, he was in a sense a captive (1 Samuel 27:1-7).

It is only natural that the malicious plots against David caused him to fear. However, through much prayer and supplication in entreating God for mercy, he trusted in God and overcame his fear. No matter how difficult the circumstances, David resolved to trust God and "praise His word" (56:4, 10), and thus he stood strong upon the Word of God without fear. He took comfort in knowing that God watches over him, and his tears touched the heart of God. He knew that 'if God was for him, who could be against him?' (Romans 8:31). Therefore, he had no fear. He could proclaim with faith that when he was safe and delivered from his enemies, he would keep his vow to the Lord by offering Him the sacrifice of praise. Once God had saved and preserved him from falling, then he could be confident that he would walk in the light (have new life) (56:13b). When Jesus saves our souls from destruction, we too can walk in His Light (John 8:12).

Prayer for today: *We cast all our burdens upon You, dear Lord, for You care for us and are touched with the feelings of our infirmities. We praise You for the supernatural peace You give which is beyond our understanding.*

Read Psalms 57, 58 &59   *May 10*

Key Verse: 57:3b *"God shall send forth His mercy and His truth."*

Psalm 57 and the preceding psalm are quite similar in style as well as content (both express utmost confidence in God); therefore, it is probably a continuation and the occasion of the psalm, as mentioned in the title, is when David had fled to hide from Saul in the cave of Adullam after leaving Gath (1 Samuel 22:1). Psalm 57 begins with the same words as Psalm 56, but here David's cry for mercy is because Saul and his men are seeking to kill him, and yet he had done no wrong (see 59:3-4).

Although David is hiding in a cave, he knows his real refuge is under the shadow of God's wings. Those lions who seek to swallow him up will first have to fight and defeat God to get at him, but that is impossible! David is also aware that God is not finished with him yet, for God had chosen and anointed him to be king; therefore no fatal harm could possibly come to him. David had the faith to call upon his Lord, saying, "God Most High...who fulfils his purpose for me" (57:2, N.I.V.). God is sovereign and providentially works all things out for the good of his children who trust in Him. How would God save David? "God shall send forth His mercy and His truth" (57:3b). Sending Jesus into the world was the greatest evidence of God's mercy, and Jesus was the embodiment of God's truth, through whom He brought the ultimate salvation to mankind: the salvation of souls.

Even though David was amid great danger, he could still sing forth beautiful words of praise to God. The God who was the Creator of the heavens and earth is exalted far above these wonderful manifestations of His glory (57:5-7). After considering God's greatness, David feels secure and his heart is steadfastly fixed upon God. Like a firmly rooted tree, even though a storm rages around him, he cannot be moved, since God has planted him (cf. 55:22). These thoughts make David want to praise God with his whole being and sing out God's mercy and truth to all people. He wants to "awaken the dawn" by shouting joyfully about the salvation of God.

Psalm 58 is a lament of David over the prevalence of injustice in the judicial system of the land. With sarcastic words, David strongly condemns the corrupt judges who have made a mockery of the Law, perverted justice, and hurt the spread of godliness in the land. Their words are like poison that slowly kills. Like all mankind, they were born with original sin, but they have not committed themselves to the redemptive work of God; so their tendency to sin has continued on unchecked since their childhood. Therefore they have become wicked, having hardened their hearts to the voice of conviction within their consciences (58:.3-5).

With righteous indignation, David repeatedly curses the perverted judges who do not deserve to live. He proclaims that God's wrath will come upon them quickly and unexpectedly. They might be cooking food and preparing to eat, but before they taste of their labour, God's burning wrath will come upon them like a whirlwind, and they will no longer be in the land of the living (58:9). With this fierce judgment of the wicked, the righteous will be glad to see the will of God accomplished. By this, all the world will know that there is indeed a God who stands in judgment of the earth and that wickedness will not prevail, but the righteous will prevail and be rewarded.

In **Psalm 59**, David urgently cries out to the Lord to deliver, defend, and save him from the bloodthirsty men whom Saul had sent to assassinate him. David, however, protests of his innocence, for he had done no wrong. The wrong was with Saul, who was jealous of David and his popularity (59:3-4). Saul's violent, unscrupulous men were likened to despised scavenger dogs. In those days, the pagans (Gentiles) were commonly referred to as dogs; therefore, these men might have been foreign mercenaries. They stalked David's house, waiting for their prey to come out, but David had been forewarned and, with the help of his wife Michal, the daughter of Saul, they devised a plan for him to escape (1 Samuel 19:11-17). These immoral men of Saul did not fear God, so they behaved without restraint. God, however, laughed at their folly and futility, for one day they would be judged and see His wrath (59:7-8). David believed he would be delivered and live to see them consumed (59:10b). Yet David asked that they not perish too quickly; he wanted their lies to be exposed and for them to serve as examples, that all might see their misery and know that God reigns supremely and will indeed judge wickedness (59:11-13).

The evil men growled and howled, wanting to satisfy their thirst for blood, but David joyously continued to sing praises to God and thank Him for His "mercy in the morning" (59:16). On that particular morning, Saul had planned to have David killed (1 Samuel 19:11a), but God intervened and delivered David. The words that David worshipfully expressed about God is true for all God's children: He is our defense, refuge, strength, and mercy (59:16-17).

Prayer for today: *Thank You, dear Lord for the security we have in You. There is no place safer than in Your everlasting arms. May we learn to rest there despite our circumstances.*

Read Psalms 60, 61&62   May 11

Key Verse: Psalm 60:12 *"Through God we will do valiantly..."*.

In **Psalm 60**, we learn of the turmoil that was in the land when David became king. It was common in those days for there to be uprisings against a new monarch; so David was forced to engage in battle against three different surrounding countries simultaneously, as we learn from the title of this psalm (cf. 2 Samuel 8:3-6, 13-16; 1 Chronicles 18:5, 12-15). While David was fighting in the north against Mesopotamia and Aram Zobah (Syria), he was attacked from the far southeast by the Edomites who thought to take advantage of the situation. David dispatched Joab and Abishai with some troops, and they won a tremendous victory. By the time the title of this psalm was written, they had a reported amount of 12,000 Edomite casualties, but the final historical records show there were actually 18,000 (2 Samuel 8:13; 1 Chronicles 18:12).

The psalm reflects Israel's attitude before the outcome of the battles were known. Israel is demoralized and in a state of panic and despair. They cannot understand the adversity against them. They feel abandoned by God. Actually, these battles proved beneficial for Israel, because they were victorious and their strength increased. David realizes that the time of despairing and complaining is over, for it only does harm. He turns to speak positively and declares that since they fear God and are loved by Him, they will march under His banner for the sake of the truth; and because they are God's people, and God Himself had laid claim to the land (2 Samuel 7:9-10; Genesis 15:18-22), their salvation and victory over their enemies could be assured.

The Lord honoured the two most outstanding tribes: Ephraim (from Joseph), having great military strength and considered the pride of Israel (cf. Hosea 7:8-10; Genesis 49:22-26) and Judah, the seat of justice and authority (cf. 78:67-68; Genesis 49:10). Their territorial inheritance was the Lord's, but here the Lord also claims Moab, Edom, and Philistia and makes the inhabitants to be servants of His people. David exclaims that without God's help their military efforts are futile. Only God could help them take the naturally fortified "strong city" of Edom which was built upon the cliffs (modern day Petra, 60:9-11; Obadiah 3), and it would be vain to ask the help of alliances (60:11b). The faith-filled exclamation of David, "Through God we will do valiantly", was indeed fulfilled.

Psalm 61 is the prayer of David when he was in exile, likely due to the rebellion of Absalom. His heart is overwhelmed with grief and loneliness, longing to return to the tabernacle of God in Jerusalem. With the feeling of despair and weakness, David pleads for God to lead him to a place of safety, a rock that is too high for him to reach and too high for his enemies as well. Today, when we make the same request, God will lead us to the Rock, Jesus Christ, where one can find eternal safety.

David recalls the many times in the past that God had been a refuge for him, and this gives him strength and assurance for the present time, as well as hope for the future. He resolves to trust in God and is sure God has heard him and will grant his longings: to have fellowship with God (abide in His tabernacle forever, 23:6; 27:4-5) and to be protected under His wings. With confidence, the psalmist believes that he and others who fear God will receive their promised inheritance, for they are heirs of the Lord (cf. Romans 8:17). Based upon God's mercy and truth, king David also believes that God will give him a long life, as well as an enduring dynasty, which was fulfilled in the Messiah, Jesus Christ (2 Samuel 7:16). His confidence in God's deliverance makes him determined to keep his daily vow of offering unto God the sacrifice of praise.

Psalm 62 is a song of total confidence in God as David's sole help and all-sufficiency. David uses his own trust in God to serve as an example and exhorts others to also trust in their divine refuge (62:8). It is a psalm of contrasts between the behaviour and trust of the righteous (62:1-2, 5-7) and that of the wicked (62:3-4, 9-10). David expresses his complete trust in God alone. His quiet spirit waits on God for his salvation, for his only hope is in God (62:1, 5). Since God is his Rock, he knows that the storms of life cannot uproot him nor shake his faith. In contrast, the wicked will easily fall and perish, because they harm others and are hypocrites. They are not steadfast upon the Rock but are lighter than vapours, because they trust in oppression, robbery, and riches. The increase of riches is not condemned for those who come by it honestly, but David's concern is that the people not set their heart on riches, for that is in vain. In summary, David proclaims God's power and mercy, which are in complete balance when it comes time for God to "render to each one according to his work" (62:12; Matthew 16:27; Romans 2:6-10).

Prayer for today: *Thank You, dear Lord, that we do not fight our battles alone. When we place our total trust in You, You honour Your Word and bring total victory to us, especially over our chief enemy, Satan.*

Read Psalms 63, 64&65   May 12

Key Verse: Psalm 65:4 *"Blessed is the man whom You choose, and cause to approach You..."*.

Psalm 63 is yet another psalm that was likley occasioned by David's escape from Absalom. It beautifully illustrates David's love for God and his close relationship with Him. David put prayer and praise as his top priority. He continually longed to be in God's presence, enjoy fellowship with Him, and see the manifestations of His power and glory from within the Holy Place; this was what motivated him to wake up early in the morning. He felt as though he desperately needed the Lord to quench his thirst and fill him, that he might have strength and satisfaction (cf. John 4:14; 6:35); and if he did not have this daily fellowship with God, he felt like a dried up desert (63:1). He needed communion with God as often as he needed water, and therefore seven times a day he lifted up his soul in praise to the Lord (119:164). If any believer wants to keep in close fellowship with God, they too must resolve to put time with the Lord at the top of their priority list.

David declares that God's lovingkindness (steadfast love and mercy) is more precious to him than his own life, yet while living he would live to praise the Lord. His sentiments are similar to those of the Apostle Paul: "For to me, to live is Christ..." (Philippians 1:21). The grace of God working in the lives of His children gives us the most important kind of sustenance: satisfaction to our souls and joy in our hearts (63:5). Therefore, like David, let us resolve to closely follow God (63:8).

Psalm 64 is a familiar plea of David for divine help and protection. There is no indication that David is in danger of physical harm, but he complains about the activities of his enemies who are working underhandedly with "bitter words" to maliciously slander his reputation and undermine his ability to rule the nation, so he might lose the support of the people (642-3). Therefore, the occasion for this psalm was likely the beginning of Absalom's insurrection, when the rebels schemed secretly rather than openly, opposing king David. David's intuition told him that soon they would suddenly shoot at him without fear (64:4), and yet, speaking with prophetic authority, he expresses his confidence that God would retaliate on his behalf with divine arrows of His wrath. When the people, who may have been indifferent to God, would finally see His great deeds in throwing down those wicked men who were once in high places, then they will rethink their position before God, come to fear Him, and become witnesses for Him. The sorrow that the righteous once had, because of the wicked people's oppression, will turn into gladness of heart, because they glorified God and trusted in Him.

Psalm 65 is a refreshing poetical song of praise to God for His goodness and bountiful blessings upon the whole earth. It was likely occasioned by an abundant harvest season, which the psalmist recognizes as a direct blessing from God. David had made a vow to daily praise the Lord, no matter what the circumstances, and as he went to the tabernacle which he had constructed to house the Ark upon Mount Zion, he proclaimed that his praises to God were awaiting expression. David knew that his God is a God who hears all the words uttered from the mouths of his children (65:1-2). How wonderful it is to know that our prayers are indeed heard by the One before whom all flesh will one day kneel (65:2) and "confess that Jesus Christ is Lord, to the glory of God the Father" (Philippians 2:10-11). He is the One through whom God has provided atonement for our transgressions (65:3), and though David did not have the fuller revelation of God concerning the Messiah, he did know that the salvation of the soul comes from God and that He would indeed make provision to atone for man's sins.

The one cleansed from the stain of sin is truly blessed and is chosen by God to approach Him like a priest (1 Peter 2:9), — have fellowship with Him, and thus receive full spiritual satisfaction (65:4; cf. Numbers 16:5). As the psalmist dwells upon the goodness and blessings of God for him personally, his mind turns to consider the goodness of God to all the earth, over which He is sovereign, and as such He is the Saviour for not only Israel but all people of the world. He who can still the waves can just as easily still people's confusion and violence (65:7). Our Lord Jesus did just that when he walked upon the earth doing the will of God (Matthew 8:26).

Because of God's grace, God gives good gifts to all His creation, such as the rain, grain, and even fertile land (cf. Matthew 5:45; Psalm 104:14, 28). There is no "mother nature"; there is an all-powerful God who is in control of nature. He is the One who gives a plentiful harvest, and so it is He whom we all should thank. As the psalmist proclaims: "You crown the year with Your goodness, and Your paths drip with abundance" (65:11). God's goodness causes nature, as well as man, to rejoice.

Prayer for today: *Dear Father, we long to be continually in Your presence, as did David. Thank You for choosing us to have fellowship with You through our Lord Jesus Christ.*

Read Psalms 66 &67 May 13

Key Verse: Psalm 66:20 *"Blessed be God, who has not turned away my prayer, nor His mercy from me!"*

Psalm 66 is the nation's song of thanksgiving to the Lord, probably written in response to a great military victory that the Lord had given His people. It invites not only the children of Israel but all the earth to shout and sing joyful praises to God, and it bears witness to His greatness (cf. Isaiah 37:20; Revelation 15:3-4). It gives us the essence of true praise: that which honours, glorifies, and magnifies God by reflecting on His divine nature and attributes (66:2-3).

A second invitation is given for all to see the marvelous works of God, which causes everyone to stand in awe and give glory to Him. David recalls two historically important, supernatural events that display the power of God: when He parted the Red Sea for the Israelites to cross over after leaving Egypt; and when He dried up the Jordan River that His people might cross over into the Promised Land (66:6; Exodus 14; Joshua 3). The power with which He rules is so great that one day all nations will come into submission to Him and praise His name. Therefore, it is far better that nations bless and fear the God of Israel now, so they too might enjoy His blessings in the present time.

Speaking from his personal experience of trials and as the nation's representative, David testifies to God's work in the life of believers on their journey of faith. The Lord sustains our life, proves us through testing, refines us through fiery trials (represented by fire and water, 66:12; cf. Isaiah 43:2), but then brings us to a place of fulfillment and abundance. In the process, we become stronger in the faith, purer, freer, and better disciplined like a good soldier who is an overcomer and a victor. Believers, then, can expect trials, but be encouraged because God has a purpose (for further study see: 1 Cor. 10:13; 2 Cor. 4:17-18; 6:3-12; 11:23-33; Romans 5:3-4; 8:18; James 1:2-3, 12; 1 Tim. 2:3-4; 3:12; 1 Pet. 4:12-19).

David utters yet a third invitation; this time it is to all who fear the Lord. With a personal testimony, David tells of how God answered his prayers and had mercy upon him, which would not have been possible if he had harboured sin in his heart. For God to hear and answer our prayers, there must be no iniquity (perversity) in our lives, for sin separates us from God (Isaiah 59:2; 1:15-18). Since God is holy, pure, and perfect, we can only come before Him if we have clean hearts — when our sins have been forgiven and are covered by the blood of Jesus — then He hears our prayers and we can enter into His divine fellowship and grace (John 9:31; 1 John 1:9; Proverbs 28:13; Psalm 32:1).

The authorship of **Psalm 67** is not given in the title but is most likely a psalm of David. Some commentators believe it was sung during the harvest season on the occasion of the Feast of Pentecost or the Feast of Tabernacles (67:6). It is a brief and beautiful heart-felt psalm of thanksgiving. It begins with a familiar benediction (cf. the priestly blessing of Aaron, Numbers 6:24-26). The psalmist, however, has adapted it to show Israel's mission; they are to be the witnesses of God to the whole world, so that the Gentiles will also find salvation from God.

In order to properly reflect God to others, they prayed firstly that He be merciful to them. It is only because of God's mercy and grace that we experience salvation, and then He bestows blessings upon us, which include His divine favour of shining His light upon us, giving us guidance, enlightenment, and strength; this, in turn, allows us to see clearly, that we might walk along the straight and narrow path without stumbling and lead others into His light (for further study see Psalm 27:1; 36:9; Daniel 2:22; John 1:4-5, 9; 8:12; 2 Cor. 4:6;1 John 1:5, 7; 2:8-11; 1 Tim. 6:16; Eph. 5:8, 13; 1 Pet. 2:9; Matt. 5:14-16).

The psalmist calls for all people on earth to praise God and sing for joy. What is the reason for their joy? It is based upon God's righteous judgment and His guidance (67:3-4). When will all people praise Him? When Jesus Christ returns to rule and reign over the earth. For the present time, however, the missionary mandate is still in effect, as it was in the time of David. He prayed for God's continued blessing upon himself and others within the covenant, so they could perform their mission of proclaiming God's name to the ends of the earth. Their goal was to preach, teach, and reach people of every nation, that they too might come to know and fear the one true God (Acts 1:8). With faith, the psalmist declares "the earth shall yield her increase" (67:6), which most likely refers to a spiritual harvest of souls.

Prayer for today: *We praise You today, dear Lord, for Your mercy. When we deserved only eternal death, You provided a way to eternal life. As was David's goal, may we strive to proclaim this Good News to all people.*

Read Psalm 68   *May 14*

Key Verse: Psalm 68: 34 *"Ascribe strength to God; His excellence is over Israel..."*

Psalm 68 is a poetic song celebrating God's many victories of the past, present, and future. It is a unique and complex psalm wherein there are passages which can be interpreted historically, theologically, symbolically, and prophetically. The occasion for composition was likely when David brought the Ark of the Lord from the house of Obed-Edom up to Mount Zion in Jerusalem (historical interpretation, 2 Samuel 6:12-15). The procession of the Ark to its resting place in Jerusalem is dramatized by the journey of the children of Israel from Egypt to the Promised Land (symbolic interpretation). This same event symbolized the ascension of God (His presence represented by the Ark) as the conquering King to His throne in the Holy and Royal City to reign sovereignly (theological interpretation). It also has Messianic significance, for the Apostle Paul quotes verse 18 as referring to Jesus Christ's ascension into heaven (prophetical interpretation).

This psalm of celebration begins by the lifting up of the Ark by the priests. The psalmist's words echo those of Moses as the Ark would set out before the children of Israel in the wilderness (v. 1; Numbers 10:35). When the presence of God arises in our midst, then no enemies of the Lord can be present; they flee and are scattered like smoke, or they will perish as wax disappears under fire (cf. Hosea 13:3; Micah 1:4). The righteous, however, are made exceedingly glad by the presence of the Lord, and are compelled to sing and praise His Name.

As the joyous procession of the Ark begins (v. 4), the people sing and extol God, whom they understand to be not confined within the Ark, for He "rides on the clouds", and the exaltation and reverence given to Him is evident by the use of His personal Name "Yah". God's majesty is such that the psalmist is inhibited and feels unworthy to use the full form of His Name, "Yahweh".

Although God dwells in His Holy habitation, He is not so high above the clouds that He is too far removed to see and care for His people; on the contrary, He watches circumspectly and helps the helpless, defends the defenceless, brings comfort to the lonely, and sets the prisoners free (Exodus 22:22-23; the ministry of Jesus, Isaiah 61:1-3; Luke 4:18; John 14:18). Those who rebel against God, however, will not prosper, just as the children of Israel who rebelled against God had to remain in the wilderness to see their death in the dry land (vv. 5-6; Hebrews 3:12-19). Yet the Lord was gracious to His people, for they were His inheritance. He marched before them as they journeyed through the wilderness (pillar of fire/cloud). With manifestations of His power, He gave them the Law at Sinai. He sustained them when they were weary and blessed them like a "plentiful rain" with manna, water from the rock, and quail (vv. 7-10). The Lord's goodness was further expressed by giving His word for Moses to write (the Law, the covenant), which was loudly proclaimed and affirmed by all the people once they entered the Promised Land (v. 11; Joshua 8:32-35).

As the procession of the Ark continued, the psalmist likens it to the victorious conquest of Canaan, as the Lord went out before them and routed the kings of the opposing armies (v. 12). With poetic imagery, the psalmist describes the riches that God's people obtained from the spoil, even though they lived in humble camps; they were like doves (simple and common birds) adorned with gold and silver (v. 13). In scattering the mighty kings of the land, God did what seemed impossible, just as snow on Zalmon is impossible, but not beyond the power of God to do (v. 14, Zalmon is a heavily forested hill near Shechem, cf. Judges 9:47-48).

Inspired by the ascending of the Ark up Mount Zion, the psalmist expresses that the most beautiful mountain of Bashan (Hermon in the north) is no comparison to the hill of the Lord's dwelling (Deuteronomy 12:5). From Mount Zion, the location of the Lord's temple (tent of meeting), the Lord's presence, glory, and power is displayed as it had once been on Mount Sinai. This makes Zion unique, for the Lord chose to dwell there, but even more unique is the fact that He dwells in us; believers are the temple of the Holy Spirit (1 Corinthians 3:16; Ephesians 2:22; Colossians 1:27).

In its resting place, the Ark represented God's ascension on high, like a conquering King upon His throne who reigns over subjected nations that bring him tribute (v. 18), such as Egypt (crocodiles, calves) and Assyria (bulls; vv. 29-31). To the people of His kingdom, He gives good gifts, and those who belong to Him escape death (v. 19-20, receive eternal life), but His enemies are found, even though they are in far or obscure places, and they are destroyed (v. 21-23).

The psalmist recalls the grand procession of the Ark accompanied by joyous music (v. 25; 1 Chronicles 13:8) and the leaders of all the tribes; however, mention is made of only the southernmost tribes of Benjamin and Judah, as well as the northernmost tribes of Zebulun and Naphtali. This procession was watched by those of other nations (v. 24), who are also invited to sing praises to God, for He is mighty, awesome, sovereign, transcendent, and faithful to give "strength and power to His people" (v. 35).

Prayer for today: *Dear Lord, as the Ark of the Covenant, representing Your presence, was brought to rest in Your holy Temple, may we daily invite Your presence in us as temples of Your Holy Spirit. As did Israel, we invite Your presence with praise and thanksgiving.*

Read Psalms 69, 70&71   *May 15*

Key Verse: Psalm 70:14 *"But I will hope continually, and will praise You yet more and more."*

In **Psalm 69**, David has reached the depths of despair. He feels he is on the brink of destruction and can only cry out to God for help. In this psalm, it is especially clear that David was a type of Christ; many aspects of his life foreshadow that of Christ. Some verses are clearly Messianic and have been quoted in the New Testament as relating to the sufferings of Jesus, but other portions of the psalm relate only to the psalmist.

Terrible persecution had taken its toll on David. He had many hateful and powerful enemies who sought to destroy him, and yet it is without cause, for he has done no wrong; yet he must pay the penalty. Jesus confirmed the prophetic interpretation of this passage by saying that this was spoken of Him (69:4; John 15:25). Truly Jesus had not sinned, yet he payed the punishment for our sins. The next two verses, however, apply only to David, who had behaved foolishly and had fallen into sin. He prays that he will not be a stumbling block to others (69:5-6).

The reproach that David experienced foreshadowed the reproach of the Son of David, Jesus Christ, and it was for the sake of righteousness: "the reproaches of those who reproach You have fallen on me" (69:9, 10, 20; Romans 15:3). Those who are against God will naturally be against the righteous who serve God. David's zeal, like the zeal of Jesus for the House of God and true worship of God, angered those who were more liberal or secular (69:9; John 2:17). Just as David had become a byword and was shunned by his own people and even his family members, so it was with Jesus (69:8; John 1:11; 7:5; Mark 3:21). David spoke poetically in saying he was given vinegar and gall, meaning he was treated with contempt and bitterness, but this was literally fulfilled with Jesus (69:21; Matthew 27:34, 48). David's reaction to his enemies, however, is in sharp contrast to that of Jesus (69:22-28). David himself had confessed that the mercy of God far exceeds the mercy of man (2 Samuel 24:14). David had prayed that his enemies be destroyed without forgiveness, but Jesus prayed for God to forgive His enemies (Luke 23:34).

With expectancy, David prayed for the Lord's salvation and his own restoration, which would cause others who were righteous to rejoice, just as the righteous, who love the name of Jesus, rejoice at His resurrection and enthronement. The prayers of the meek (poor) shall be heard; their hearts shall live (eternally), and they shall dwell in the heavenly Jerusalem to praise Him forever (69:29-36).

Originally, Psalm 70 & 71 may have been one single psalm. With the exception of a few minor variations, **Psalm 70** is the same as Psalm 40:13-17. The psalmist, David, likely made use of his earlier composition and altered it for a specific occasion and purpose. David is aware of his own inadequacy to help himself out of a desparate situation. He describes himself as "poor and needy" (70:5). As a prosperous king, he certainly did not lack in anything, but he lacked the ability to save himself. All his life he had trusted in God for deliverance and magnified the Lord in all situations, and now is no exception. He has a source of strength that is far greater than himself, so he calls upon God — his only help in trouble.

In **Psalm 71**, we read of David's familiar request that he not be put to shame. Why was David always so concerned that he not be ashamed by seeing defeat? It was not so much for himself, but for the sake of God, since, as a righteous king, David was God's representative. If he was put to shame, it would reflect badly upon the Lord, but David sought to always glorify the Lord. Upon being delivered, David would publicly worship God and give God all the credit, as he had done numerous times over the years. In such a way God would be glorified. David also repeatedly prayed for his enemies to be put to shame and suffer in a state of confusion, so that none of their schemes would work against him (70:2; 71:13); for that too would bring glory to God, since they were against God, and it would show that the righteous side was victorious. At the close of this psalm, David joyously praises God for answering his prayers (71:24).

David was quite old at the time of writing this psalm, and he had known much adversity during his life, yet since his childhood, he maintained a close relationship with God, and now that he is near the end of his life, he is even closer to God. He declares that since his birth God had upheld him (71:6) and taught him (71:17), and all his life he had declared God's wonderous works and goodness. Now that he is old, he resolves to do the same, as well as to praise God more and more and continually hope in Him (71:14). He prays that God would grant him a long enough life to teach the present generation all that God had taught him, and to tell them of God's power, strength, and righteousness (71:18-19). David is determined to make his latter years very productive in God's service, and with faith believing, he proclaims that God will revive him, restore his honour, and give him comfort so that he might continue to sing praises to God and witness to others about God's righteousness all day long (71:20-24).

Prayer for today: *Our desire, oh Lord, is to draw closer to You every day and praise You more and more. As Your representatives, may we reflect Your goodness to others and never put You to shame.*

Read Psalms 72&73   May 16

Key Verse: Psalm 73:24 *"You will guide me with Your counsel, and afterward receive me to glory."*

Psalm 72 is one of the two psalms ascribed to Solomon in the title (the other being Psalm 127). The final verse of this psalm indicates that this psalm is the last within the second book of the prayers of David, but does not necessarily indicate Davidic authorship. It appears that it is a hymn to be used at the cornation of a descendant of David in Judah. However, from the contents it is clear that no earthly king could ever fulfill all the beautiful words spoken. Jewish tradition understood this psalm to be Messianic, as did the early church. It depicts the peaceful reign of the Great Son of David, Jesus Christ. Kingship was not only determined by descent, but by divine appointment, for Israel was under a theocracy (rule of God), and her kings were subjected to the Great King. Since Jesus was from the House of David, He had an inherited right to kingship, as well as divine authority to be King. The Messiah's reign will be the only truly righteous reign, since God will govern. All people will be judged impartially, and there will no longer be any oppressors (72:1-4).

Christ's universal dominion (millennial reign) will be characterized by peace and the flourishing of the righteous, for all will fear

Him. There will be continual prayer and praise to Him and an absence of enemy uprisings — therefore, no war. All nations will be subjected to Christ; they will worship and bless Him. He will care for the needy, so there might be no needy people, but there will be an abundance for everyone. Only of Jesus Christ the King can it be said that His name will endure forever and the whole earth will be filled with His glory (Philippians 2:9-11). What a glorious hope we as believers have in Christ Jesus!

Psalm 73 was composed by Asaph, one of David's Levitical choir leaders, whose songs were later sung by the Levitical choir during Hezekiah's reign (1 Chron. 15:16-19; 2 Chron. 29:30). He was struggling with the prosperity of the wicked and the sufferings of the righteous (also dealt with in the Book of Job and Psalm 37), yet he knew that those whose hearts were clean before God (and not merely ceremonially clean) were blessed by God (73:1). Even so, he nearly slipped in his faith, for he felt offended and angered when he saw that the wicked were enjoying wealth and getting wealthier. They were healthy and lived at ease, even though they were proud and did not fear God, nor did they even believe God could see and hear them; they were so ungodly that they questioned His very existence (73:11).

Doubts had crept into the psalmist's mind about his own spirituality. Was it worthwhile? Does it make any difference? He thought for a moment that he might be better off if he went the way of the wicked (73:13-14). He knew, however, that as a spiritual leader, he was responsible to his generation and it was painful for him to even imagine a whole generation lost because of his rash words; so he dared not voice his doubts and complaints lest he lead anyone astray (73:15). The troublesome dilemma stayed with him until he took his concerns to the Lord in prayer within God's sanctuary, where he would have worshipped God and meditated on His Word. This was the turning point. Finally he was enlightened! He understood that God's justice and judgment would be dealt out to the wicked in their latter end when they would perish (73:18-20; 27), and it was only because of His grace that He did not consume them immediately.

The psalmist was now no longer envious but grieved because of his foolishness and carnal mindedness in doubting the importance of following God's ways and living a pure and righteous life. He realized that with God's continual guidance and counsel (by prayer and meditating on God's Word), God would one day receive him to glory. What a remarkable revelation about heaven and eternal life, the hope of glory for the believer! The psalmist now resolves to trust in the Lord and draw closer to Him, that he may be a witness for God (73:28).

Prayer for today: *Dear Lord, we know that one day You will come to rule and reign, bringing perfect peace and filling the whole earth with Your glory. May we keep an eternal perspective in this present life, causing us to rest in You and reach the lost.*

Read Psalms 74&75 May 17

Key Verse: Psalm 74:12 *"For God is my King from of old, working salvation in the midst of the earth."*

In **Psalm 74** we read of the destruction of Jerusalem, as well as the desecration and burning of the Temple. The title of this psalm tells us that Asaph was the author, but a problem arises when one considers that during Asaph's life (a contemporary of King David) there was no destruction by an invading enemy in Jerusalem; this did not happen until centuries later by the Babylonians under Nebuchadnezzar (2 Kings 25:9-10; 2 Chronicles 36:19). There are two possible explanations: a descendant of Asaph (an Asaphite) wrote it at the time of the invasion whose name may also have been Asaph; or the original Asaph of David's day wrote it prophetically, which is quite possible, since he was known as a seer (a prophet who sees visions of the future, 2 Chronicles 29:30).

The psalmist is totally bewildered by the destruction he sees in Jerusalem, and he cannot understand why God has allowed this to happen to His sheepfold, unless they were terribly guilty of horrendous sins. Asaph is perplexed by what seems to be God's abandonment of His people. He cries out for God to remember His inheritance whom He had redeemed as His own out of their bondage in Egypt (74:2) and to remember the covenant He had made with Abraham to give his descendants the land (74:20).

What is even more bewildering to Asaph is how God could allow the enemy to destroy His own dwelling in Zion! At that time, when one nation conquered another, it was believed that their gods were more powerful than the God or gods of the enemy. Therefore, their prime target was to deface or destroy the temple of the opposing God or gods and set up the emblems (standards/banners) of their gods and their nation to show they were victorious (74:4). It was heart-rending for Asaph to see in ruins the most beautiful building dedicated to their Lord. All the exquisite carvings were defaced by their axes (74:6; cf. 1 Kings 6:29). Asaph understands this to be a mockery of God. He asks God to remember how the enemy has blasphemed, reproached, and rebelled against him, that He might vindicate Himself by consuming all the wicked fools (74:22). Asaph, however, knows that the God who is powerful enough to part the Red sea, dry up the Jordan river, destroy the Leviathan from the face of the earth (see Job 41 which deals with history many centuries earlier), make a rock into a fountain (Exodus 17:6), create the earth and establish night and day, winter and summer, is certainly able to destroy any foe (74:13-17). The psalmist's hope is restored when he proclaims that his God is the King of the world who has a plan of salvation for the earth (74:12).

It is significant that in **Psalm 75** the questions posed in the preceding psalm are answered. Asaph is also ascribed as the author of this psalm. He begins with a prayer of thanksgiving to God who is not so far removed that He is unconcerned about the affairs on earth; His past gracious dealings prove He is near (75:1). Asaph received the answer to the question he had asked God: "how long will the adversary reproach [You]?" (74:10). The Lord proclaims that He will indeed bring judgment, but it will be in His own perfect timing, according to His plan (75:2). God further proclaims that no one upon the earth will be able to withstand His righteous judgment. He is all-powerful, the One in whom all things have their being and without His grace in setting up "its pillars firmly", the earth would collapse (75:3). The Lord warns the boastful to not be conceited and stiff-necked (arrogant, proud, obstinant). To the wicked He says, "Do not lift up your horn on high", like a beast that attempts to use its power against someone, which is what they were trying to do to God (75:4-5). These types of people exalt themselves, but Asaph rebukes them in saying that there is no place on earth where they will receive exaltation. Only God, the Sovereign Judge, will decide whom to exalt and whom to put down (cf. 1 Samuel 2:7; Daniel 2:21). Since He knows the hearts of all people, He also knows who is to be punished with His cup full of wrath, which He will pour out upon the wicked until the very last drop (75:8). Once again, the Lord speaks to warn that the horn (strength, power) of the wicked will be cut off, but the strength and power of the righteous will be exalted, and they will live to sing praises to the righteous King.

Prayer for today: *Thank You, Father, for Your way of salvation You have planned since the beginning of time. May we walk worthy of our high calling in Christ Jesus and tell others of Your great plan and judgment to come.*

Read Psalms 76 & 77   *May 18*

Key Verse: Psalm 77:12 *"I will also meditate on all your work, and talk of Your deeds."*

Psalm 76 is a song of Asaph or possibly one of his descendants. We read of the Lord's deliverance of His people and protection of His royal city of Jerusalem (Salem/Zion). Psalm 75 prepared the way for the Lord's judgment of wrath on the proud, wicked enemies of Israel, and Psalm 76 shows the administration of that wrath. The situation described may be referring to the Lord's miraculous victory over the Assyrian army of Sennacherib, who had laid seige to Jerusalem and whom God had caused to die in their sleep (2 Kings 19:35). In this psalm we see that the Lord only had to speak the words of rebuke and all the mighty men were cast into a sleep of death (76:5-6). It reminded the psalmist of God's great deliverance for the children of Israel when they escaped from the Egyptians who, along with their chariots and horses, perished in the deep waters (76:6; Exodus 15:23-28). Their many arrows, shields, and swords were rendered useless (76:3; compare Isaiah 37:33). These weapons and all the possessions of the strong men were plundered by the people of the Lord. The reaction of both Judah and Israel (possibly indicating that it was indeed during the time of the divided kingdom) was one of great praise to God, for the strong enemy had been defeated by the Lord alone.

All over the earth, the Lord is to be feared, for He is so great. No one can endure His wrath (76:7; cf. Nahum 1:6). Even the wrath of men against God will ultimately bring Him praise and glory (cf. Romans 9:17, 22-23). When those who are against God are destroyed, all the saints of the Lord will offer Him their thanks and glorify Him. The proud rulers of the earth will be humbled before the awesome and majestic Great King, who is mighty in deeds of deliverance for His people (76:12). This particular deliverance of the oppressed people of Judah represented the great deliverance yet to come when God will bring judgment and "deliver all the oppressed of the earth" (76:9). The worldly view says, "God helps those who help themselves", but the Bible teaches: "God helps those who cannot help themselves." God's miraculous intervention on behalf of the oppressed, who were totally dependant upon Him, deserves not only verbal praise but active worship to God in sacrificial giving: "make vows to the Lord your God, and pay them" (76:11).

In **Psalm 77**, Asaph relates his personal experience of great distress. He begins by telling us the outcome when he cried out to the Lord: "He gave ear to me" (77:1). That which begins in prayer will usually end in praise and victory. Asaph reflects upon his desperate situation and the many questions going through his mind; then he remembered the Lord's past goodness, and it gave him new-found faith and strength.

In recalling his trouble, Asaph remembers that he went right away to the Lord in prayer, and he continued to pray with his hands outstretched to God all the night, yet he found no comfort, and this is what puzzled him. After all, he was a child of God and a faithful keeper of the covenant. When he remembered God's past mercies, he was even more perplexed at why God would not answer him now, and he complained against God. Because of his troubles, he could not sleep or even speak. After remembering his former close relationship with God, he resolves to make a careful search of his heart (77:2-6). Obviously, Asaph's initial prayer to God was not done with the right attitude.

He asked six rhetorical questions about God's faithfulness and character (77:7-9). Recognizing that God is indeed faithful to His covenant and that His mercy and grace endures forever, the psalmist realized the problem was not with God but with himself: "This is my anguish [infirmity]" (77:10). His healing was well on the way when Asaph decided to meditate upon God's many wonderous deeds and glorify Him. He would do more than meditate, however; he would unselfishly tell others about the Lord's goodness. Asaph's faith increased when he remembered God's gracious deliverance of His people in parting the waters, which trembled at His presence, making a path for His people to cross the Red Sea. By this time, Asaph had faith that God would likewise lead him out of his troubles, and he was now in the proper spirit to receive an answer from God, no longer having a complaining spirit.

Prayer for today: *Lord God, when we hit bottom in deep despair, may we not pray out of complaint but meditate on Your wonderful deeds of the past with thanksgiving in our hearts. Then Your peace, which passes all understanding, will come in answer to our prayers (see Philippians 4:6,7).*

Read Psalm 78   *May 19*

Key Verse: Psalm 78:38 *"But He, being full of compassion, forgave their iniquity, and did not destroy them."*

Psalm 78 is an historical psalm entitled, "A Contemplation of Asaph". It is a psalm of instruction as well as a warning for the people of Judah to follow the Lord faithfully and not make the mistakes of their forefathers. These warnings also apply to us today (1 Cor. 10:1-12; Hebrews 2:1-4). Asaph, a contemporary of David, traced Israel's rebellious history and God's merciful dealings with them. He urged the people, as did Moses, to pass on their spiritual heritage to successive generations by telling their children of God's wondrous deeds and teaching them His Law (cf. Exodus 10:2; Deuteronomy 4:9; 6:7). Asaph gave them several reasons why this was important, and it is still relevant today: (1) that the oral transmission may continue to the next generations; (2) that they might have trust and hope in the Lord, for faith comes by hearing (Romans 10:17); (3) that they might not forget the works of God — His merciful redemption; (4) that they might keep His commandments; and (5) that they might not be stubborn and rebellious like their forefathers, but rather set their hearts on God and be faithful to Him.

Another purpose for Asaph's discourse was to illustrate why God rejected the northern tribes (represented by Ephraim, v. 67) and chose Judah instead as the recipient of His promise. Ephraim was renowned for its good soldiers who were always anxious to engage in battle, but in the spiritual battle for the Lord they were renegades, even though they had been armed with the teaching of God's Law. They did not keep the Lord's covenant and were unfaithful, because they did not instruct their children in the Law nor tell them about God's miraculous deeds; therefore, they "forgot His works" (78:10).

In order to remind the people, Asaph describes God's works in detail, giving special attention to the greatest event of Israelite history: the Lord's miraculous deliverance of His people from bondage in Egypt. After describing the exodus, Asaph tells of the nation's experience in the wilderness. He showed how God graciously guided and gave them sustenance (water from the rock, manna, quail), even though they continually complained against him, tried his patience ("tempted God"), sinned against Him, doubted Him, acted hypocritically, and did not keep the covenant. We also read that they "limited the Holy One of Israel" (v. 41). The Hebrew word translated as "limited" is better rendered as "vexed", which led to the limitation of the work of God because of their lack of faith and unbelief. Several times, God's wrath burned against them, but because of His compassion, He forgave them and did not wipe them off the face of the earth (v. 38).

Asaph explained how the people were apostate and idolatrous during the time of the Judges, and he uses the metaphor of the "deceitful bow" (that causes one to miss the mark — a meaning of the word "sin"). Asaph is referring mainly to the northern tribes, for Ephraim was symbolized by the bow (v. 57; cf. Genesis 49:24). The Lord demanded their sole allegiance, so when they turned to worship idols, He was moved to jealousy. From this point in the psalm, we read of the Lord's reaction. The tabernacle had been erected in Shiloh, a city within the inheritance of Ephraim (Judges 18:31; 1 Samuel 1:3, 24), but God forsook His tabernacle when He allowed the Philistines to conquer and take the Ark of the Covenant (vv. 60-61; 1 Samuel 5:1). He also ordained that the corrupted priests die in the battle (v. 64, 1 Samuel 4:11). At that time, however, the Lord was gracious to raise up Samuel, the one to anoint David from the tribe of Judah (v. 68), for God had chosen the tribe of Judah to fulfill His promise of redemption. Just as God had guided His flock by the hand of Moses and Aaron (77:20), He now chose David to be the shepherd of Israel; but the greatest Shepherd from the tribe of Judah who came to fulfill God's promises was Jesus Christ, our Lord and our Shepherd today (Hebrews 13:20).

Prayer for today: *We praise You, oh God, for delivering us from sin through the Blood of Christ and for being so patient and merciful during our times of complaining. Help us to faithfully pass on a godly heritage to our children and grandchildren.*

Read Psalms 79&80   May 20

Key Verse: Psalm 80:19 *"Restore us, O Lord God of hosts; cause Your face to shine, and we shall be saved!"*

Psalm 79 is closely related to Psalm 74. Both were composed by Asaph and deal with the terrible destruction of Jerusalem, which had been prophesied (79:1-2; Jer. 9:11; Micah 3:12) and later fulfilled by the Babylonians (2 Chronicles 36:16-20). Psalm 74 is mainly a lamentation for the destruction of the city, but Psalm 79 concentrates more on the destruction and persecution of the people.

The main purpose of the psalm is to plead for God's divine justice, in order to bring vengeance upon their enemy (79:6, 12). They asked that He be their blood avenger since the enemy had killed many of God's saints and shed innocent blood (79:2-3; 10b; cf. Deut. 19:11-13). They based their request upon the compassion and mercy of God, who would hear the groaning of the survivors and preserve those whom the enemy had appointed to die (79:11). Their first order of business, however, was to ask God to forgive them of their iniquity, for they recognized that the calamity was because of their sin and the wrath of God upon them (79:5, 8). They reasoned that those who did not know God and had never called upon Him should receive even a greater portion of God's wrath (79:6).

Another reason the people of Judah asked for God to destroy the enemy was that by allowing these idolatrous people to remain the victors, it brought shame and reproach upon the people who served

God. The fact of greater importance, however, was that it brought reproach upon God, and they were concerned that God's name be glorified. They did not want to see the neighbouring heathen nations question God's existence and mock Him because of the destruction of His people (cf. Ezekiel 25; Obadiah 12). They prayed: "For the glory of Your name", "help", "deliver", "save", "and provide atonement for our sins" (79:9). When they would receive this and see God's retribution upon their enemies, then the sheep of God's pasture said they would give Him praise and thanks forever.

The Levite Asaph had a burden in his heart for the salvation of the Northern tribes, particularly the Joseph tribes of Ephraim and Manasseh. In **Psalm 80**, he pleads that God would be their Shepherd. The occasion of the psalm, however, appears to be after the division of the Kingdom, therefore the author may have been a descendant of the Asaph, unless he wrote it himself prophetically. The distressful situation portrayed here seems to be when the Northern Kingdom was defeated by the Assyrians and carried away captive (2 Kings 18:9-12).

Asaph petitions God to once again show His favour ("cause Your face to shine") so that His lost sheep might be saved. The psalmist's love for these desparate tribes causes him to identify himself with them and give voice to their prayers of repentance: "restore us, O God" (80:3; cf. Jeremiah31:18). Interestingly, each time this same refrain is repeated, the name they use to call upon God reveals that they are drawing closer to Him. In the second refrain, they call Him "O God of hosts" (80:7), recognizing Him as a mighty God who is victorious in bringing deliverance. In the third refrain, the personal name of their covenant God is used, "Yahweh", usually translated as "Lord" (80:19).

As in Psalm 79:5, the defeated Israelites ask God: "How long will You be angry? (literally "smoking"; 80:4). They wonder when all their prayers will finally stop God's wrath from fuming against them. They are like a vineyard that has been burned with fire at the mere rebuke of God, because His countenance had ceased to shine upon them (80:16; compare 44:3). If the vine does not receive the sunshine upon it, it will perish. The reason God did this was because His high quality vine had degenerated (cf. Jeremiah 2:21).

The metaphor of the vine has often been used for Israel (cf. Isaiah 5:1-7; Hosea 10:1; Luke 20:9ff), and Jacob used it for the Joseph tribes of Ephraim and Manasseh (Genesis 49:22). Asaph shows how God had nurtured His people as a caring vinedresser, who transplanted them from Egypt to Canaan and caused them to take root in the Promised Land and cover the large area from the Mediterranean Sea to the Euphrates River (80:11). Now, however, the walls around them have fallen and foreign beasts have entered, plundered, uprooted, and destroyed the vine (80:12-13). Asaph calls upon God to once again visit His vine and revive it, making special mention of the branch (Ephraim) that He had once made very strong (80:15).

What was the answer for this desparate and degenerate vine? Jesus came as the true vine for all the degenerate people of the world. He was what Asaph called "the man of Your right hand" (cf. Heb. 1:3; 10:12; Acts 7:56) and the "son of man" (Matt. 18:11), whom God would make strong for Himself (80:17). The branches of the vine are now all those who believe in Jesus, and if they abide in Him they will have life and be able to bear fruit (see John 15:1-11). He is the Light of God, and because He shines within us, "we shall be saved!" (80:19).

Prayer for today: *Thank You, Father, for the restoration You have made available through Christ for all degenerate mankind. We pray that our new life in Jesus, the vine, will bear fruit as we reach out to others with Your love.*

Read Psalms 81, 82 &83　　*May 21*

Key Verse: Psalm 81:13 *"Oh, that My people would listen to Me, that Israel would walk in My ways!"*

Psalm 81 was likely composed by Asaph, the musical Levitical choir leader who was a contemporary of King David. The psalm is a liturgical hymn that may have been used on the occasion of one or more feasts, such as the Passover, the Feast of Tabernacles, or the Feast of Trumpets. We read a descriptive account of the opening ritual of the feast that was accompanied by an assortment of musical instruments, as well as the blasts of the trumpet, or ram's horn (*shophar*), at specific times according to the lunar calendar. Asaph declared that it should be done in the prescribed way, for it was a law of God (81:4; Numbers 10:10).

With a prophetic utterance, Asaph speaks the words of God, who declares how He had freed His people from bondage in Egypt and gave them water from the rock at Meribah (81:7b; Exodus 17:6-7). He warns them not to turn to idolatry, for He has proven Himself to be their all-powerful God in whom they have all they need. Like trusting sheep, they need only open their mouths and the good Shepherd will feed them. If people today would only listen to Him (81:8) and obey Him, then they too would have all they need to fill their empty hearts and souls. God is truly our all-sufficiency!

Sadly, the Lord continues to tell how His people did not listen to Him. They persisted in doing evil, and so they suffered the most fearful of punishments — being given up to their sins without the restraint of His grace upon them (81:11,12; Romans 1:21-28). The Lord longed that they would return to Him, for if they had, they would have enjoyed only blessings and victory instead of curses and defeat.

In **Psalm 82** Asaph rebukes the corrupt judges of his day. He warns that the Lord God stands to oversee every courtroom (2 Chron. 19:6-7). He brings judgment upon the judges, who are called "gods" because they are overlords in lofty positions (cf. John 10:33, 34-38). The judges were favouring the wicked and not giving justice to the common person, which implies that they were taking bribes. A judge in Israel was to represent God, so theirs was a great responsibility. Like God, they were to defend, give justice, and save the needy from the oppressors (82:3-4; Deut. 1:17). Only Jesus was one just Judge who rightly represented God. Truly these unjust, corrupt judges walked in darkness (82:2), and their sin was so great that Asaph felt it shook the very foundation of society (82:5); this is so true, for if the justice system fails, then wickedness goes unchecked.

Asaph further warns that although they are important, wealthy, and prestigious, in the end they will die like any other man and "fall like one of the princes" (82:7). A "prince" often symbolized the tyrants of the land, so if one behaves treacherously, they will ultimately suffer the treacherous conquences (Hebrews 9:27). There is hope, however, for on an appointed day in the future, God will arise to judge the earth, and the great King, our Lord Jesus, will inherit all nations and rule righteously (82:8).

Psalm 83 is a prayer for God's protection from hostile neighbouring nations that were conspiring together against Israel. The most probable occasion was during the reign of Jehoshaphat when Moab and Ammon ("the children of Lot", 83:8; Gen. 19:37-38), the principle powers, formed a coalition and invaded the Southern Kingdom of Judah. Allied with this coalition was Edom, Syria, and others that are not mentioned by name in the Chronicles account but likely include some or all of the nations mentioned in this psalm (83:6-7; 2 Chronicle 20:1-2, 10-11). Interestingly, one of the sons of Asaph named Jahaziel, was moved upon by the Spirit of the Lord to declare that the battle is the Lord's and they need not fear (2 Chron. 20:14-17). He may well have been the Asaphite author of this psalm, for to have such faith in God's deliverance he likely spent much time in prayer that God would not "keep silent" (83:1) but "pursue", "frighten" (83:15), and "let them be confounded and dismayed" (83:17). As the history in 2 Chronicles records, this prayer was indeed answered, for God put the enemy in such confusion that they fought against each other and perished (2 Chron. 20:22-24).

In the psalmist's prayer, he referred to the many victories that God had given Israel during the time of the Judges, such as those against the Canaanite and Midianite coalitions (Judges 4:15-24; 7:25; 8:12). If God could win these victories, the psalmist was encouraged that God would do it again, and in so doing He would shame the enemies. The psalmist voiced God's ultimate goal in the destruction of the wicked: that these heathen nations may know that He alone is the Most High God and that they might seek Him and experience His salvation (83:16, 18).

Prayer for today: *You, oh God, are our all-sufficiency, and You long to bless and deliver us if we will but listen to You and obey. We yield our stubborn wills to Your leading. Use us today, we pray.*

Read Psalms 84&85 — May 22

Key Verse: Psalm 85:9 *"Surely His salvation is near to those who fear Him, that glory may dwell in our land."*

Psalm 84 is the song of a pilgrim who is full of expectancy and happily making his way to Jerusalem to worship and give praise to the Lord. He is full of intense longing to be in the wonderful, peaceful Tabernacle. For him, one day at the tabernacle is better than living a thousand years. To serve God in the humblest position as a doorkeeper is better than living luxuriously with the wicked (84:10). It seems from the way he speaks that he had been in the Tabernacle before but had been away from it for some time and his whole being was yearning to return (84:2).

This psalm is surprisingly similar in tone and perspective to Psalm 42 and 43, which were also composed by a Korahite (they served as musicians and some as gatekeepers; 1 Chron. 6:33-38; 9:19). In Psalm 42 and 43, the psalmist is sorrowfully leaving his land, possibly as a captive. Could it be that Psalm 84 was composed by the same man who is now returning to the Tabernacle in answer to his faith-filled prayer request (43:3-5)? It is a beautiful thought. We know that the Lord is indeed faithful, and He does answer prayer.

Like the birds that had made their homes in the sanctuary precincts, the psalmist desires to do the same, that he might always be close to the presence of God. He knew that the man who dwells in

God's house is blessed, having continual communion with Him, forever praising Him, finding strength in Him, serving Him, and trusting Him. "Blessed" can be translated as "happy", for he receives good things from God, such as His grace and mercy. For such a person as this, who walks uprightly, the Lord is a sun and shield, for he experiences the light of life and the protection of His presence (84:11).

While on the pilgrimage, the psalmist and those accompanying him, would pass through "the Valley of Baca", which literally means "weeping". It was likely a long and dangerous journey, full of troubles and sorrows yet the Lord sustained and strengthened them and the dry land became like a spring with abundant water (cf. Isaiah 35:7; 48:21). God saw that all those faithful pilgrims reached their destination, that they might worship the Lord together (84:7; Heb. 10:25), just as He will for those of us today who will one day be in His presence in glory.

Psalm 85 is a song of great emotion and a prayer for revival. The psalmist remembers God's mercies and goodness. Once he had not shown favour to His land, nor to His people; but then His anger turned and He forgave His people of their sin, which was the cause of all their troubles, leading to their captivity and exile. It is possible that this psalm refers to the Babylonian captivity of Judah and their return (Jer. 29:14; 2 Chron. 36:20-21). Although the Lord had brought them back and forgiven them, they were still in need of physical and spiritual revival, for they were in a poor condition (cf. Nehemiah 1:3). When sin is present, it naturally brings about the wrath of God. The righteous psalmist longed for God to look upon His people only with pleasure not with wrath, so they might rejoice in Him.

After his prayer, he paused to hear what the Lord would answer. He was confident that God would speak peace. There would come a time when God would look upon His people with only pleasure, but they must be careful to "not turn back to folly", which implies moral failure (85:8). Truly, as the psalmist foresaw, salvation was near for those who fear God. God gave the psalmist a prophetic message, and he envisioned a time when mercy, truth, righteousness, and peace would meet together in close union upon the earth, which would be a time of great blessing (cf. Isaiah 32:16-18). This time will only be realized when our Lord Jesus comes to rule and reign over the earth as is portrayed in Psalm 72. In Him is righteousness, and in His footsteps we will be guided (85:13).

Prayer for today: *We pray, dear Lord, for a mighty revival in our land today. Cause all people to acknowledge and fear You, as You make Yourself real to them. Use us for such a purpose in the last days.*

Key Verse: Psalm 86:9 *"All nations whom You have made shall come and worship before You, O Lord, and shall glorify Your name."*

Psalm 86 is a prayer of the master psalmist, king David. It is an emotional expression of a godly soul who makes many requests to the Lord. Throughout the psalm, he asks that the Lord would hear, preserve, save, show mercy, teach, deliver, strengthen, and show him a sign. With every request, he gives a reason why he believes the Lord will answer Him, and voicing these reasons builds his faith. The first basis for his faith is because his pleas are based on personal necessity. He admits that he is needy and oppressed, and he knows that God defends and helps the helpless, for he has experienced God's help in the past (86:13,17b).

Secondly, his pleas are based upon his faith relationship to God. The psalmist is set apart and consecrated to God ("holy" 86:2). He is the Lord's child and His servant. He also trusts in God, has lifted up his soul to God, and walks in His truth. Because of David's faith, he worships God by offering Him praise and thanksgiving with his whole heart and by giving Him glory.

The third reason the psalmist is confident that God will answer his cry is based upon God's divine nature. David has a close relationship with the Lord, and therefore knows the Lord's character. From the many references in this psalm to the writings of Moses, we know that David was familiar with the Law, and knowing God's Word, along with prayer, is the best way to draw closer to Him. The psalmist is certain God will answer because He is good and "ready to forgive" (86:5), "full of compassion, and gracious, longsuffering and abundant in mercy and truth" (86:15; cf. Exodus 34:6). There is none other like Him. The gods of the heathen are merely imaginary. He alone is God who does great and wondrous things and has a redemptive purpose for the whole world (86:8-10; cf. Exodus. 15:11).

Psalm 87 is a remarkable little gem that is unique in the Psalter. It is an expansion on the thought of Psalm 86:9, which foresees the salvation of people from every nation. Psalm 87 may have had an historical background, such as the favour Israel received by other nations in Hezekiah's day (2 Chronicles 32:23), but the main interpretation of this psalm is prophetical. The psalmist envisions Zion as the capital of the Kingdom of God, which cannot be explained geographically but rather spiritually (Hebrews 11:10; 12:22; 13:14; Revelation 21:10). It is the new Jerusalem that has been founded and built by the Lord; therefore, the Holy City is sanctified and her gates are loved by God (87:2; Isaiah 60:11). Glorious things are spoken of Zion, which could never be said of any earthly city, even though it be very beautiful (e.g. Isaiah 2:3; Psalm 46:4-5; 48:1-3).

Those from nations that were historical enemies of Israel, such as Egypt ("Rahab"), Babylon, Philistia, and Tyre will come to know the Lord and have their names written in the Lord's register. There will also be those from distant places that make Zion their home, who are represented by Ethiopia/Cush (cf. Isaiah 18:7). All people, whether Jew or Gentile, who know the Lord Jesus will be equal citizens and receive the same privileges (Ephesians 2:18-19; Colossians 3:11; Philippians 3:20). Their unity will be found in the Lord, and Zion will be the mother city for all who are born of God, having experienced the second birth from above through faith in Jesus Christ (John 3:3-6; Galatians 3:8; 4:26; Rev. 7:9). In the City of God, all inhabitants will enjoy the spring, which is the source of joy and life (87:7).

Psalm 88 is a personal lament of a man named Heman, whose identification is uncertain but may have been one of David's chief musicians (1 Chronicles 15:17-19). This is yet another unique psalm. It is unlike the laments of David, in that it is one of deep despair without any expressions of hope or praise to God. The way Heman expresses his turmoil is very similar to the way David spoke when he called upon God in distress; therefore, Heman was likely familiar with the psalms of David. If he was indeed the levitical singer, he would have sung many of David's compositions.

Heman has been sorely afflicted since the time of his youth and believes it is the wrath of God upon him. He feels that if God does not intervene soon, he will die; therefore, his desperate cry reflects the extreme urgency of the situation. He prays that God would let him live, that he might continue to praise Him, but he has a very limited understanding of the afterlife. He may have been suffering from a contagious skin disease such as leprosy, which would make him unclean, and that would account for why his family and friends were kept far from him (88:8, 18), and this is the sad note upon which the psalm ends. Although words of faith and hope are not expressed, the fact that Heman cried out to God day and night is in itself evidence of faith, for he knew his only hope was in God. Therefore, he could cry out: "O Lord, God of my salvation..." (88:1).

Prayer for today: *Dear Lord, we know that one day soon every knee shall bow and every tongue confess that You are Lord, but for many this confession will be too late. We pray that Your Holy Spirit would empower us and give us wisdom to win souls for you.*

Key Verse: Psalm 89:1 *"I will sing of the mercies of the Lord forever; with my mouth will I make known Your faithfulness to all generations."*

Psalm 89 is a lament over the downfall of the Davidic dynasty. The psalmist pleads for God to restore it according to His promise. The identification of the psalmist, named Ethan, is uncertain, but he may have lived at the time when Babylon defeated the southern kingdom of Judah and when king Jehoiachin, a decendant of David, was put to shame and taken prisoner while still in his youth (vv. 38-45; 2 Kings 24:8-16). The psalmist, however, knew of God's covenant with David to give him an enduring dynasty; in fact, he quotes a condensed version of the promise the Lord spoke to David (vv. 3-4; 2 Samuel 7:11-16).

Ethan is concerned and yet confident, because he knows that God is faithful and full of loving-kindness which had been proved over and over again by His delivering the nation in the past, such as from Rahab (a name which refers to Egypt). He also knows that nothing can be compared to God, who is the Creator and sole Sovereign over the whole world. Those who serve Him and know the joyful sound of His praises are blessed with the light of His countenance upon them and are thus continually joyful, strengthened, and exalted by Him, as was king David (vv. 14-18). Ethan affirms that the foundation of God's throne is righteousness and justice, and that mercy and truth are His emissaries (v. 14). God could never have spoken falsely to David, and therefore the psalmist believes that God will indeed fulfill His promise to David; but he was confused to see that there was no longer a king from the line of David reigning in Jerusalem.

The promises of God to David, His chosen and anointed one, have been fulfilled in the great Son of David, Jesus Christ. He was the ultimate "anointed one" (meaning "Messiah") who came as the first-born of God (Rom. 8:29; Col. 1:15, 18; Heb. 1:6; 12:23; Rev. 1:5) and who cried out to Him: "You are My father" (vv. 26-27; John 17:1, 5, 11, 21, 24-25). With the fuller revelation of God in Jesus Christ, we understand how God fulfilled His promise to David, but the psalmist could only hope and pray. Ethan understood that God was chastising the sons of David, but he also knew that His loving-kindness would not be utterly taken away, for the Lord declared, "My covenant I will not break", and truly, God cannot lie (v. 34). The big question in Ethan's mind, as is often seen in the psalms, is: "How long, Lord?" (v. 46). When would God's wrath cease? All they could do was wait expectantly for the salvation of the Lord, which later came to be their hope for the

Messiah. Truly, God did not break His covenant with David. The first chapter of the New Testament shows how Jesus the Messiah was the Son of David, and the early church taught that He was the fulfilment of God's promises in the Holy Scriptures (Romans 1:2-4).

Prayer for today: *Thank You, Father, for the precious promises You have given us in Your Word, which You are always faithful to keep. We desire today to sing Your praises and declare Your faithfulness to a world that knows the heartache of only broken promises.*

Read Psalms 90&91   May 25

Key Verse: Psalm 91:14 *"Because he has set his love upon Me, therefore I will deliver him; I will set him on high, because he has known My name."*

Psalm 90 is unique because it is the only one in the psalter ascribed to Moses, and although it is a personal meditation, he speaks on behalf of the whole nation. Moses probably wrote this during their wilderness wanderings, when they had no place to call their home and were very susceptible to enemy attacks. Moses learned, however, that their safe dwelling place was in God.

When Israel sinned in not trusting God to enter Canaan, after reaching the border, God's wrath was upon that whole generation (with the exception of Joshua and Caleb), and they were excluded from entering the Promised Land (Num. 14:19-35). During those forty years of wilderness wandering, they saw many, many people die, which constantly reminded them of their sin and of man's frail, transitory nature; man is here one day and gone the next, but God is from everlasting to everlasting. God has neither a beginning nor an end, for He is our eternal God who is above time (2 Peter 3:8). Man, however, is bound by time and his lifespan is very short and fleeting, even when one lives beyond his seventy years and reaches eighty (90:10).

Considering the shortness of our days, Moses concludes that each day is precious and should be spent gaining wisdom in our hearts. The biblical definition of wisdom is to fear God, that is, to revere, respect, and obey Him with a sincere heart (Prov. 9:10). If we labour daily to know God, love Him more, and abide in Him, then our days will not be futile; they will find satisfaction in God's mercy and be filled with rejoicing (90:14).

Moses concludes by asking that God would bless them by letting His work, glory, and beauty be upon them and their children.

He also asks that God would establish all the work of their hands — something especially important for their children who would inherit the Promised Land. Moses knew that without the Lord going before them into the Land, they could never succeed (90:16-17; cf. Deuteronomy 2:7; 14:29; 16:15; 24:19).

Since **Psalm 91** is untitled, it is traditionally believed to be composed by the author of the preceding psalm; therefore, this may well be another psalm by Moses. It expands upon the thought of Psalm 90:1, which expresses that the Lord Himself is "our dwelling place". In Psalm 91, we learn of the blessings received by those who **abide** in Him. There is a difference between one who dwells and one who abides in the Lord. To dwell means to remain for a time, but abide means to continually remain or stay. Not all believers abide in constant closeness and fellowship with the Lord, but this is what He desires of His people. This difference in the closeness to God could account for the drastic change in tone from Psalm 90, which is somber, to that of Psalm 91 which is joyful and comforting (compare 90:10 and 91:16).

The blessing in this psalm is the security of the one who trusts fully in the Lord. He is providentially protected from "the snare of the fowler" (one who traps birds), which means that the believer who abides in the secret place of the Lord will never be caught in a trap by the great liar and deceiver, Satan. Under the wings of God, the trusting believer finds a place of refuge like a well protected chick (91:3-4a).

Another means of protection is in knowing the truth of God (His Holy Word), which acts as our armour, that we might be victorious over evil and never have fear (91:4b-6). Yet another means of protection for the one who abides in the Lord is that God's angels will keep watch over him, lest he stumble (91:11-12). Satan quoted this verse of scripture in tempting Jesus, but since Jesus knew the truth of the Word of God, He knew that Satan twisted its meaning. When Jesus rebutted by quoting the truth of Scripture, it was like a weapon, whereby Jesus was victorious (cf. Heb. 4:12; Eph. 6:17). The devil left and the angels came and ministered to Jesus (Matthew 4:5-11). Those who abide in the Lord and know His truth, can likewise be victorious over the devil and his demons, and the angels are close by to come to our aid. Whether it be a lion (an open and direct attack by Satan), or a serpent (an indirect, deceptive, or subtle attack by Satan) the abiding believer will trample over it victoriously (91:13)!

God Himself gives the reason for all these blessings: "Because he has set his love on Me...[and] because he has known My name"

(91:14). The fuller revelation of God in the New Testament has revealed that name to be "Jesus". Therefore, to know God's name is to know and love Jesus personally and abide in Him (Acts 4:12; John 15:4-9). Our Lord Jesus is that refuge — "the secret place of the Most High" (91:1; Heb. 6:18-20).

Prayer for today: *We love You today, oh God, because You have first loved us and have proven Your love in so many wonderful ways. Teach us the secret of abiding in You, giving us a place of peaceful rest and security.*

Read Psalms 92, 93 &94   May 26

Key Verse: Psalm 92:12 *"The righteous shall flourish like a palm tree, he shall grow like a cedar in Lebanon."*

Psalm 92 was used in the Temple liturgy on the Sabbath, likely during the special offerings (Numbers 28:9). This psalm celebrates the righteous works of the Lord and testifies to the prosperity of the righteous. We learn the importance of giving thanks to the Lord individually and corporately for His loving-kindness and faithfulness as well as His sovereignty over creation and righteous judgments.

The psalmist is not troubled by the prosperity of the wicked as were Job (Job 21:7) and Asaph (Ps. 73:2-3). He understands those to be fools who do not fear God nor consider His way, and although the wicked are numerous, they will soon be destroyed like the temporal and easily withered grass. In contrast, the wise man does consider the profoundness of God (92:5; cf. Isaiah 55:8-9; Romans11:33). He recognizes that God is "on high forevermore" (92:8) and His enemies will perish. He is likened to two trees: a flourishing palm that represents honour, strength, continuity, and fruitfulness even in its old age; and a cedar of Lebanon (Is. 2:13; Ps. 104:16) which is always green, tall, of top quality (its wood was used for the temple), and firmly rooted, so that it can withstand all storms. These blessings are from God who exalts and strengthens His servants who flourish in His presence (92:10, 13; 27:4-6) so that they might be able to be effective witnesses for Him by declaring God's righteousness and strength (92:15; cf. Deut. 32:4).

Psalm 93 describes God as the transcendent, mighty, Sovereign Ruler and Eternal King over all creation. Many of the psalms which follow also proclaim that God reigns as King (95:3; 96:10; 97:1; 98:6, 9; 99:1). Just as He is from everlasting to everlasting (90:2), so His throne is established for eternity (93:2). Unlike an earthy king, whose garments merely represent majesty and strength, the Lord Himself is clothed with majesty and strength. His kingdom has no boundaries, for He is not only sovereign over Israel (Deut. 33:5; Ex. 15:18) but the whole world (Isaiah 24:21-23; Rev. 19:6), and since it is established by Him, it cannot be shaken by any opposing force (93:1; cf. Heb. 12:28).

The ungodly nations which ruled and often oppressed the earth are represented in this psalm by the "floods" (literal translation is "rivers"), such as the great empires or world super powers which are often symbolized by the Nile River (Egypt) and the Euphrates and Tigris Rivers (Babylon and Assyria; Jer. 46:6-8). Though they should rise up like a torrent against God and try to destroy His plans, all their attempts are futile (94:11), for God cannot be shaken (29:10). These empires will themselves be washed away, but God's House (Kingdom) will remain forever, since it is based upon His attributes, such as His holiness (93:5; 47:1-3; cf. Isaiah 66:1; Acts 7:48-50). His testimonies are a great treasure which will also remain fixed and sure forever because they are truth (cf. 19:7-9).

Psalm 94 gives a message of comfort and consolation to the righteous in the midst of affliction and persecution by oppressors. God's people know, without any doubts, that God rules with all authority over the earth, and yet when they see evil men mocking the righteous, they are anxious for God to give them their just deserts. The people of God do not ask for this out of bitterness or enmity, but it is a cry for vengeance or retribution (cf. Jer. 51:56), so that evil will be gone and the evildoers, who do not fear God, will be punished with what they deserve (Rom. 6:23). The righteous call for God to "shine forth", asking that He reveal Himself (50:2; 80:1) with His divine authority, for wherever the brightness of God's glory shines, there can be no evil.

The evildoers are proud, arrogant, insolent people, who may have been apostate Jews or Gentile foreigners. They praise themselves for their evil, and they are so treacherous that they take pleasure in afflicting and even murdering the orphans, widows, and strangers who were helpless; but under the Law of God, they had rights in Israel (Ex. 22:21-24). Even though the crimes committed were against the Law of God and the sacredness of their fellow man, they still continued to sin, since they imagined that "the Lord does not see" (94:7; 10:11; Ezek. 8:12; Isa. 29:15; Luke 8:17; 12:2-3). The psalmist calls them the most foolish of people (94:8; 92:6). How could they believe that the Creator could not see their wrongdoing or hear them (94:9)? God can even see into the heart and minds of man, since He has all authority and is greater than His creatures (139:1-4; John 2:24-25).

The psalmist turns to testify about the providential and personal care God gives him which provides peace of mind and inner rest in the midst of turmoil. He also affirms his belief in the power and righteousness of God and the final retribution of evil as God judges the innocent blood they spilt. The righteous can take comfort in knowing that evil will not go unpunished.

Prayer for today: *Thank You, Lord, for the promises You give to Your righteous servants. Help us to grow tall and strong in You, like a firmly-rooted tree, and bear fruit for Your eternal Kingdom.*

Read Psalms 95, 96&97   May 27

Key Verse: Psalm 95:3 *"For the Lord is the great God, and the great King above all gods."*

Psalm 95 to 100 form a group of songs composed for liturgical and congregational use. They have a common theme. They are all theocratic psalms which speak of the sovereignty of the Most High God, who reigns as King. They have Messianic significance. They hint at the reign of Christ and they all begin with the call to praise the Lord, but each one is distinctive. Some of the older translations of the Bible ascribe their authorship to David, and the writer of the Epistle to the Hebrews alludes to the Davidic authorship of Psalm 95 (Heb. 4:7).

Psalm 95 is a beautiful expression of the people's worship to God. Verses one through seven may have been sung by the common worshippers or the levitical choir in their procession to the Lord's House. They magnify the Lord by proclaiming His greatness in being their rock of salvation, as well as recognizing Him as the only true God, who is not only the great King over the whole world but the omnipotent and omnipresent Creator of everthing and thus worthy to be praised (Rev. 4:11; Heb. 13:15).

In verses six and seven, the joyful group has arrived at the place of worship, where they are struck with awe and reverence before the presence of the Lord. They invite others to show their respect by bowing down low and kneeling before their great God and Creator. Their actions and attitude signify their humility, total loyalty, and submission to Him.

In the midst of their worship, the Lord gives a warning to them that is a continuous challenge for all believers of every generation. They are to guard their hearts from turning hard as did their forefathers at Meribah (meaning "contention" or quarrel"), and at

Massah (meaning "temptation", "test", or "trial"; Exodus 17:1 – 7) who had seen the mighty works of God and still doubted God's ability to bring them into the Promised Land; so God caused that generation to not enter His "rest", which represents the ultimate rest for all believers (Num. 14:21 – 23; Deut. 1:26 – 39; 12:9; Heb. 3:7 – 4:11).

Psalm 95 was a national hymn, but **Psalm 96** is a missionary hymn with a universal vision. King David spoke these words at the time when the Ark of the Covenant had been brought to Jerusalem (1 Chron. 16:23 -33), which supports the Davidic authorship of the psalm. It invites people of every nation to be involved in singing praises, blessing the Lord, and daily "proclaiming the good news of His salvation" and His glory and wonders (marvelous deeds) to every heathen nation (96:2-3).

The God of Israel, who made heaven and earth, is to be praised and feared above all other gods, since they are false and merely man-made idols of stone or wood (96:5; cf.Ex. 18:11; Isa. 2:8, 18-20; 40:19-20; 44:9-17). God, however, is the great King, full of honour and majesty (cf. 93:1; 104:1). Strength and beauty are in His holy sanctuary, since His presence is there, as is symbolized by the Ark of the Covenant (96:6; cf. 78:61). All nationalities are exhorted to come reverently into the Lord's House to give him worship and offerings "in the beauty of holiness:, which represents the pure heart of the one who is consecrated to the Lord.

This psalm closes with a Messianic prophecy that exhorts those who know the Lord to preach to all people the imminent return of the Messiah. He will reign over the earth with justice and judge all people righteously (96:10-13; 9:8; 22:27-28). The whole realm of creation will be influenced by His coming (96:11-12; Is. 55:23; 11:1-9).

Psalm 97 expands upon the last verse of the preceding psalm. After the coming of the mighty King judge and purge the world of evil (prophetically picturing the second coming of Jesus Christ), His reign is praised by all those who benefit, since they are a part of His kingdom. This includes the people of the Lord Jesus, who are the people of spiritual Zion; it also includes the whole earth and all creatures which are made glad (97:1, 8, 11). At His coming, the glorious brightness of His deity will be veiled by clouds that surround Him, as it was on Mt. Sinai (Ex. 19:16, 18). Because He rules with righteousness and justice, He will come with an awesome display of power and sweep away His enemies and all evil with His fiery wrath, whether they be in Jerusalem or in any other part of the world (Is. 42:25; 2 Pet. 3:10 − 12). For them, however, it will not be a time of rejoicing, for they will be put to shame and will perish (Rev. 19:20). In light of this contrast, the conclusion is drawn by the psalmist that God's people, who are now being preserved by Him and have experienced His light (97:11), have an obligation: to love the Lord, hate evil, rejoice in Him, and give thanks.

Prayer for today: *You, oh Lord, are the one and only God over all the universe, and we magnify Your name today. We know Your coming is very soon and long to see Your glory. May we live in this expectancy which compels us to be a witness to others.*

Read Psalms 98, 99 & 100　　May 28

Key Verse: **Psalm 100:1** *"Make a joyful shout to the Lord, all you lands!"*

Psalm 98 continues with the theme of the Lord's righteous reign, and it opens and concludes like Psalm 96. It is simply entitled "A Psalm", but in the first verse we read that it is a "new song", which is always a thankful expression from a heart that is inspired by the goodness of God. The Lord's marvelous deeds and the victories He has won throughout the ages (especially Jesus' victory over Satan at Calvary) bear witness to all the earth of His salvation. He purposely and openly revealed His righteousness and salvation so that Gentiles may also enter into the covenant with Him (Isaiah 52:10; Rom. 10:13; Acts 1:8). To the house of Israel, He has been faithful in fulfilling the promises of the covenant and sending Jesus the Messiah to bring deliverance from sin. In Him "all the ends of the earth have seen the salvation of our God" (98:3), because He rules, reigns and judges all the world with perfect justice (98:3,9).

After remembering God's gracious mercies and His salvation, the response of His people should be one of exuberant, joyful praise to Him with a variety of musical accompaniment which adds to the joy and celebration (Isaiah 52:9). When Christ, the sovereign King, comes to establish His Kingdom, after winning the final victory, all creation will benefit. Nature will also join in praising Him (Rom. 8:19-21).

Psalm 99 is yet another royal psalm which is dedicated to the holiness of God (99:3, 5, 9). It joyfully celebrates and prophetically anticipates the reign of Jesus Christ as Sovereign King. From the beginning of the psalm, the Lord is pictured upon His great throne, which was symbolized by the cherubim atop the Ark of the Covenant, and the Mercy Seat represented His footstool (cf.132:7; Isa. 60:13; Lam. 2:1). It is to His throne room in the House of God that the psalmist invites God's people to go and worship Him (99:5). This Hebrew concept, however, did not limit God, for the Ark merely represented God's presence, and in other scriptures we see that the whole earth is considered the footstool of God (Isa. 66:1; Matt. 5:35).

From His throne on high, the Holy King establishes and executes perfect justice without showing any partiality (99:4). Even Moses, Aaron, and Samuel, who were faithful servants of God and intercessors on behalf of Israel, were judged for their sin (99:8, cf. 106:32-33; Num. 20:12-13; 1 Sam. 8:1 — 5). These were great men of God who were likely selected as examples in this psalm because they appreciated the holiness of God, and God answered their reverent prayers. With equal reverence for His majesty and on the basis of His holiness, we too should exalt and worship the Lord.

Psalm 100 closes the series of royal psalms that began with Psalm 95. It is the shortest psalm in the group, but it is the most comprehensive and profound. It serves as a closing doxology which invites all nations to joyously worship the Sovereign Lord. He alone is God, and His oneness is affirmed (cf. Deut. 6:4; 1 Kings 18:39). He is also affirmed as our Creator, which is a major basis for our obligation to praise Him (100:3), but it is more than just an obligation; we serve Him with gladness, out of the thankfulness of our hearts. The psalm praises the King of kings and Lord of lords for His continued faithfulness, goodness, and mercy. Those who love and worship Him recognize their dependence upon Him for He is their Maker. They affirm that they are His sheep who receive all they need from His pasture (cf. Isa. 43:1; Eph. 2:10; 1 Pet. 2:25; Heb. 13:20-21).

The people of the congregation of the Lord are exhorted to come into His presence where they have the privilege of thanking, praising, and blessing His name. In closing, the psalmist gives the reasons why we should "make a joyful shout to the Lord" (100:1). Firstly, because "the Lord is good"; secondly, "His mercy is everlasting"; and thirdly, "His truth endures to all generations" (100:5). When the believer considers all these wonderful things, it gives him good reason to get excited about the Lord!

Prayer for today: *Lord, when we consider Your greatness and majesty, our spirits soar in praise and worship to Your holy name. May the joy and excitement of serving You be evident to the world, that they too might taste of Your goodness.*

Psalm 101 is a pledge that king David made before the lord to rule God's people righteously. He made strong resolutions to serve as a worthy king under the kingship of God. He determined to behave wisely and blamelessly in his own house (101:2). The man who administers his home and family wisely by leading them spiritually and being a good spiritual example, will also be successful in other areas of his life (cf. 1 Tim. 3:1-5, 12). It is often much easier for people to walk uprightly and blamelessly among strangers and in public than among their own families, but David resolves to show himself upright and among those he knows best.

In his home and the courts of his palace, King David declared that no wicked thing would come into sight. The wickedness that King David was likely referring to are idols and the sin of idolatry which was so prevalent in his day. He hates the sins of the apostate, and asserts that they will have no influence on him. We, likewise, must resolve to guard our homes from any objects that might come in and have a bad influence on us, so that we can also exclaim: "a perverse heart shall depart from me; I will not know wickedness."

David is determined to eradicate wickedness from his kingdom, from Jerusalem because it is the city of the Lord, and from his own palace since he is the Lord's representative. David detests those who slander their neighbour, lie, work deceit, and who have proud hearts, for such people never humble themselves before God or the king, and cannot be trusted. They deserve to be severely punished. David would never consider such people to be in his service, for if they do not obey God, they will likewise not be faithful and obedient servants to him. Those who are faithful to God, however, will be looked upon with favour and will be raised to honoured positions in his service, for they could be expected to be faithful and trustworthy.

Psalm 102 is the only psalm with such a unique title. All other titles have either an historical or musical reference, but this one describes the condition and circumstance around its composition. This psalm is anonymous but it may have been composed by a faithful Jew who had desired to see the city of Jerusalem rebuilt after it had been destroyed but was suffering persecution from the opposition (Ezra or Nehemiah are among the possible authors).

With great urgency, the psalmist cries out to God to answer him. He feels like his days will soon be over and they are passing quickly and vanishing like smoke without accomplishing anything (102:3, 11a). He feels very much alone, as is evident from the metaphors of the solitary birds. He feels weak, wasted away and useless as the metaphor of the cut down ("stricken") and withered grass indicates (102:4, 11b). Even though he has humbled himself before God and openly showed his sorrow (covered with ashes), his enemies still reproach him (102:8-9). He believes that all his troubles are because of the wrath of God against him, for once he was in an exalted position, but now he feels like an outcast (102:10).

Thinking of his own transitory nature makes him remember the eternality of God whose Name will be known in every generation. Because of God's immutable and eternal nature (102:12, 26-27), the psalmist has faith that the time has come when God will "arise and have mercy on Zion" (102:13). The solution to the psalmist's own personal problem seems to be tied up with the Lord's mercy on Zion by building her up. Jerusalem's scattered stones are looked upon with favour as God's servants seek to do His will and rebuild the city. Confident that it will soon be accomplished, the tone of the psalmist drastically changes to joyously praising God.

In a prophetic fashion the psalmist declares the restoration of Zion and the sovereign reign of the Lord when all the kings of the earth will be in subjection to Him, and all kingdoms will serve Him (102:15-16, 21-22). At that time He will descend with justice to set the prisoners free and deliver His people from certain death (102:20). This pictures well the coming Messianic reign of Jesus Christ and such an interpretation is affirmed by the writer of the Epistle to the Hebrews who quotes 102:25-27 as referring to Jesus (Hebrews 1:10-12). He participated in the creation of the world, which will perish (Isa. 65:17), but He will never change for He is eternal (Heb. 13:8). All those who come to love, believe in, and put their faith in Jesus the Messiah will remain and be established in the eternal inheritance (89:36; Isa. 66:22; Gal. 3:7).

Prayer for today: *Father what an honour and privilege to be living in this time of Your grace. Our hearts have tasted of Your goodness and we look forward with excitement and expectation to our final dwelling place with You where justice and righteousness rule.*

Read Psalms 103 & 104　　May 30

Key Verse: Psalm 103:1 *"Bless the Lord, O my soul; and all that is within me, bless His holy name!"*

Psalm 103 is one of the most beautiful expressions of praise to the Lord penned by King David. With great sincerity and earnestness, David blesses the Lord with all his being and displays a remarkable depth of insight into spiritual things. The psalmist's words are pure and joyful, without any hints of sorrow or complaints. He speaks to his soul to remember (continually) God's many blessings (103:2). He recounts the personal benefits he has received from the Lord, and in enumerating them, he encourages others to whom these same wonderful blessings are available. The greatest blessing is listed first: God "forgives all your iniquities". He also heals our physical and spiritual diseases; he redeems our souls from destruction by the blood of Jesus; he crowns, satisfies, and renews us to be strong in Him and, like an eagle, soar over life's problems (103:3-5).

The psalmist also remembers the national blessings of the Lord, which are His righteousness and just judgments for all who are oppressed (103:6). He also mercifully condescended to reveal Himself and His ways to Moses (because of their intimate relationship), and He showed His mighty deeds to the children of Israel. The Lord is to be greatly praised for His abundant mercy, grace, and patience which was evidenced by His lenient punishment for their severe sins (103:8-10). By using many illustrations, the psalmist shows the unimaginable vastness of God's mercy, forgiveness, and paternal compassion on His weak and frail children (103:11-14).

After hearing of these marvelous benefits, which come as a direct result of God's mercy, everyone in the world would naturally want them; yet there is a condition to receiving them. The Lord's mercy and righteousness are granted only to those who fear Him and are faithful in keeping His covenant and putting His commandments into practice (103:17-18). God's greatness, goodness, and sovereignty demand the universal praise of all His creation, including the angels who obey and serve Him as messengers and agents who perform His will (103:20-22).

Psalm 104 is similar in many respects to Psalm 103. They both begin and conclude with the same words that call for David's innermost being to bless the Lord; this summarizes the basic purpose of these psalms — to glorify the Lord. Psalm 104 deals poetically with God's marvelous work of creation. He is the one pictured as not only the maker of the universe and every creature but the co-ordinator and sustainer of all His creation. He did not just create the world, wind it up, and let it go on its own; no, He watches and providentially cares for everything that happens on the face of the earth.

We read in Genesis 1:3 that on the first day of God's creative work there was light, and yet the sun and moon were not created until the fourth day. In beautifully poetic terms, the psalmist explains that the light was radiating from God Himself, and then God spread out the firmament "like a curtain" (104:2; Gen. 1:6-8). Graphic descriptions are given concerning the all-important provision of water that God gave to make the earth fruitful. When God spoke the word, the waters covering the earth obeyed and went to the places that God had founded for them, and thus He created dry land, the boundary of the water (104:6-9; cf. Gen. 1:9-10).

God provided springs and rain "from His upper chambers" to satisfy all living things (man, animals, vegetation), which is a blessing of His grace (Matt.5:45). The psalmist explains how the laws of nature (such as gravity) were ordered by God and nothing happened by chance or accident. With His creation of the sun and moon, God appointed the seasons, as well as night and day (Gen. 1:14), and His creatures live in perfect harmony as God ordained. The wild and nocturnal creatures have their domain at night, and mankind labours during the day (104:20-23).

The psalmist marvels at God's infinite wisdom in creation. He is awed by the innumerable creatures God made in the sea. Indeed, even today, new aquatic life forms are being discovered all the time. Every creature, whether in the sea or on land, is totally dependent upon God (104:27-30). He holds all things together and sustains life, for "in Him all things consist" (Col. 1:16-17; Heb. 1:3; John 1:3; Rev. 4:11). After meditating upon God's greatness (which is something we all should do), it is no wonder the psalmist resolves that as long as he has breath, he will praise the Lord, and concludes by shouting, "Hallelujah!" (the Hebrew is translated as "praise the Lord", 104:35). As we have seen, if God is in such control and cares for all creatures, how much more does He care for the crown of His creation, mankind, people who are created in His own image and so precious to Him (104:17; Matt. 6:26)?

Prayer for today: Our hearts are filled with praise, oh Lord, as we recount the many blessings You have graciously given us. It is so marvelous to think that the great Creator of all things is intimately concerned about each one of us. We long to draw closer to You today.

Read Psalms 105 &106 *May 31*

Key Verse: Psalm 105:8 *"He has remembered His covenant forever..."*

Psalms 105 and 106 are historical psalms that go together as a pair. In the former, God's marvelous and gracious deeds are emphasized. In the latter, Israel's ingratitude and disobedience are the focus. These two historical psalms would have been for congregational use. The people of Israel would always be reminded of God's goodness to them, yet warned not to behave disgracefully as had their forefathers. It was probably written during the period of the exile, when the first of the captives were returning to Jerusalem (106:46-47; Ezra 9:9; Ezra or Nehemiah are possible candidates for authorship).

Psalm 105 begins by a detailed description of what it means to praise the Lord, which includes speaking about Him as a witness to others (105:1-5). This psalm praises God for His faithfulness in fulfilling His promise to Abraham. It is addressed to the "seed of Abraham" (105:6), the chosen people who are recipients of His covenant, yet it is relevant to Gentile believers as well who, through faith in Jesus, are truly the sons of Abraham (Galatians 3:7; Romans 9:6-8; John 1:12,13). We can learn more about God and His character from the history of the children of Israel (1 Cor. 10:6, 11). God was faithful to His covenant with Abraham in bringing them into the Promised Land (105:8-11; Gen. 13:15-16; 15:18; Deut. 7:8,9), just as He was faithful to fulfill His promise of sending the Messiah from the seed of Abraham. Therefore, we who serve and love Him today can be confident that He will always remain faithful to us, His elect, and bring us into our eternal inheritance.

The psalmist paints the positive side of their history in showing how God providentially cared for His people (cf. Deut. 32:8-14). He rebuked nations and kings, and even worked in nature to preserve His people (105:14-16). The main emphasis is God's great deliverance of His people from bondage in Egypt when He sent the horrible plagues against the Egyptians so His people might go free and that He might prove Himself as the only true God (105:26-36; 106:8). With great joy, He brought them out (105:43), and with many miracles, God guided, protected, and sustained His people in the wilderness. He provided bread from heaven (manna) and water from the Rock, both of which symbolized the spiritual sustenance that Jesus brings (cf. 1 Cor. 10:4; John 6:31-35, 48-51; 7:37,38). The climax of the account is when God fulfilled His promise by giving them Canaan, in which they enjoyed the fruit of the Gentile's labour (105:44; Josh. 24:13).

With the privileges of the covenant, however, come an obligation and a responsibility. The children of Israel were to worship Him and obey Him (105:45; Deut. 4:4-8); but, in contrast to God's faithfulness (Psalm 105), we see in Psalm 106 that they were not faithful in keeping the covenant. The psalmist speaks from a repentant heart, showing the negative side of Israel's history. From the onset they rebelled, forgot His mercies and miracles, lusted, murmured, and tested God. They complained and had selfish desires, which God satisfied by sending the quail; yet because of their indulgence, they had leanness in their souls (106:14,15). This can happen today to people who are materialistic and set their hearts on the luxuries of this world; their souls suffer malnourishment.

They continually angered the Lord, but because of his great mercy, they were never punished to the extent they deserved. When they sinned with the golden calf, "they changed their glory" for an idol! (106:20). God is a jealous God. He will not share the glory that is due Him alone (cf. Isa. 42:8; Rom. 1:23). Idolatry takes many forms that are still prevalent today, and God's people must guard that they never glorify anything or anyone above God.

The people of God were to reflect His character and His light and be holy, pure, and undefiled, that they might be witnesses for Him to the heathen. However, the opposite happened. The heathen influenced them and became a snare to them. They fell into the same horrible sins for which the Canaanites in the land had been cast out. They became defiled and the land was polluted (106:37-39), so God cast them out as well. They went into the Captivity, but still God heard their cries and showed them unmerited favour and mercy (e.g. Daniel, Esther, Ezra, and Nehemiah). The psalmist concludes his lengthy confession with a request for continued mercy and restoration. Truly, as the historical examples prove, our Lord is abundant in longsuffering mercy, which He still shows, even to this generation, and for it we, like the psalmist, must remember to give Him thanks.

Prayer for today: *Thank You, Father, for being so patient with us when we grieve Your heart through our vain pursuits and foolish pride. Help us to tear down any idols in our lives that have taken priority over our relationship. May nothing hinder our daily walk with You.*

JUNE

*The "Tower of David" along the walls of the old city
of Jerusalem.*

Special Note: Be sure to write in your request today for your next volume of *DAY UNTO DAY, the Year Two — Summer* edition. It starts July 1!

Read Psalms 107 & 108   June 1

Key Verse: Psalm 107:1-2a *"Oh, give thanks to the Lord, for He is good; for His mercy endures forever. Let the redeemed of the Lord say so..."*

Psalm 107 is closely related to the two previous psalms in subject matter. They all praise God for His goodness and mercy. Psalm 107 is the answer to the prayer of 106:47, showing how God saved His people from the hand of the enemy. Isaiah 62:12 uses the same term "the redeemed of the Lord" for the children of Israel who returned from the Babylonian captivity, but a wider interpretation can also be applied. Those from all corners of the world whose souls have been redeemed by the blood of the Lamb, our Lord Jesus, have good reason to sing and give thanks to God for His goodness (Eph. 1:7).

The psalmist gives four real-life illustrations as to why the redeemed should thank the Lord for His deliverance. After each example of God's redemptive work, the psalmist repeats the refrain, "Oh, that men would give thanks to the Lord for His goodness". He does so to remind the people to thank the Lord in every situation (107:8, 15, 21, 31). The first example is of God's care over the wandering sojourners who called out to Him in their distress; he brought them out of their trouble and led them along the right path (107:7). This may be referring to some of the returned exiles at a time when God miraculously strengthened them and provided for their needs (cf. 87:5 − 7). He not only satisfied their physical need but, more importantly, their spiritual need (107:9). Within every person there is a void that only God can fill, and until He does, the soul will remain unsatisfied and longing to be filled. (Ps. 42:1, 2; 63:1,2).

The second illustration is of God's care over the captives. Those who were chained and had the sentence of death looming over them called out to God. He miraculously freed them and brought them out of darkness (107:13-14). Those who are enslaved by sin today can still be brought by Him into His wonderful light (1 Peter 2:9; Col. 1:12-13; Eph. 5:8; Phil. 2:15; Matt. 5:16). The psalmist may be referring to the people of Judah who were carried away captive to Babylon, since the reason for their affliction was "their rebellion against the words of God" (107:11). A similar divine deliverance is shown in the third illustration. Those whose souls and physical well-being were afflicted because of sin. They were on the brink of death and destruction, but the Lord graciously heard their cry; "He sent His word and healed them, and delivered them from their destructions" (107:20).

The final illustration is that of the sea traveller whose life is endangered by the stormy sea. He is totally at the mercy of God, for

119

only God can calm the raging storm; He also calms and makes glad those who cry out to Him. God guides their weathered ship to a safe haven of rest (107:30). What should be the response of all those who experience these blessings from the Lord that accompany redemption? The psalmist repeatedly exclaims that the redeemed of the Lord are to give thanks, publicly and joyously declaring His mercy and goodness in providing redemption; and they are to exalt Him before the congregation of the Lord (107:1, 22, 32). God's mercies are further expressed in His providential care of the righteous (107:35-42). If they are wise, they will understand these deeds of lovingkindness of the Lord (107:43, 22) and will naturally respond by offering Him the sacrifice of praise and thanksgiving.

Psalm 108 is a song of victory, expressing hope and confidence in the Lord, for He delivers His people from their enemies and He wins the battle. It contains portions of two previous psalms of David. Verses are taken from Psalm 57:7-11, and verses 6 to 13 are from Psalm 60:5-12, with only slight variations (for a more detailed study, see the comments on these earlier passages). One difference is that in verse 3 we find the Hebrew word "Yahweh" used instead of "Adoni", but they are both translated as "Lord". Yahweh is a more personal word that signifies a close relationship with God. Only His servants can truly call Him by His personal name. This psalm is not just a vain repetition, for such words of praise to the Lord can never be exhausted. Whether the psalmist was David himself or a compiler, there was a specific occasion which demanded such a hymn of praise in order to encourage the people. Notice that this psalm is composed of only the joyous and uplifting portions of the previous psalms. The distressing situations that David experienced before penning these words of praise are excluded. It always encourages the soul to hear positive reports and dwell on the goodness of God (cf. Phil. 4:8).

Prayer for today: *We give you praise, oh God, for satisfying our spiritual emptiness: a void only You could fill. What a privilege it is to be counted among Your redeemed.*

Read Psalms 109 & 110 *June 2*

Key Verse: Psalm 110:1 *"The Lord said to my Lord, 'Sit at My right hand, till I make Your enemies Your footstool'."*

The authorship of **Psalm 109** is ascribed to King David, who experienced much slander and treason against him by members of his court at the time of Absalom's rebellion. David is full of righteous indignation. What makes it worse, is that their hatred of him is without cause. David had done nothing against them. He had only shown them love. Those who are unrighteous will naturally hate those who are righteous, for those in darkness cannot stand the light.

It is true that David's words do not show mercy on his adversaries. They have not shown mercy to him or to others (109:16), but he takes no physical action against them in retribution. He turns to the Lord in prayer (109:4b), which is the right course for anyone who has been despitefully used. David, however, stresses the wrath of God against evil and he prays that the evil his adversaries had done would fall back on their own heads ("eye for eye, tooth for tooth", 109:17; Ex. 21:24). However, the teaching of Jesus tells us to show love and mercy to those who despitefully use us, just as He shows mercy (Matt. 5:38,39). David, however, had not attained the character of Christ, nor did he show the grace that is in Christ. This shows how imperfect man is compared to the divine nature of our Lord. David not only prays for the death of his accusers, but that their families might also suffer and perish, having no posterity to carry on their name. Having many descendants was considered a great blessing from God, but these evildoers deserved only the curses (Deut. 28:15ff).

To some, this chapter may be offensive because of its vindictive nature. We must understand, however, that this, as well as many other imprecations against the wicked (e.g. Psalm 35; 69:27,28) were because they were against God. Remember that the New Testament age of grace through our Lord Jesus had not yet come. David was still acting under the Law. As the king in that culture, David had every right to sentence these people to death as traitors. At that time it was a common thing for the traitor's family to suffer punishment or death with the traitor.

David desired that God would receive all the glory in his deliverance and that it might be a witness for God. He closes with words of confidence, believing that he will have the opportunity to praise and worship God publicly for the answer to his prayer. Truly, the Lord is the One who saves us from the great accuser. Satan, who was the father of these people, rose up against God's anointed servant David (Rev. 12:10; John 8:44).

From the onset of **Psalm 110**, it is clear this is a Messianic psalm. It is frequently quoted in the New Testament as referring to the Messiah Jesus. There is no doubt that this psalm was composed by David, since our Lord Jesus also attests that David was led by the Holy Spirit to write it prophetically (Matt. 22:43-45; Mark 12:35-37).

This psalm seems to be the continuation of Psalm 2, for it completes the prophetic account of Jesus Christ's final great victory.

From the first verse, we learn that this psalm speaks of the Messiah. Jesus taught the Pharisees this interpretation: "The Lord (Heb. Yahweh, the personal name of God) said to my Lord (Adonai, who is David's master and King, the Messiah), 'Sit at My right hand'." After Jesus' resurrection and ascension, God exalted Him by giving Jesus His rightful place of authority and divine governship, seated at His right hand (Matt.22:44; Acts 2:30-35; Eph. 1:19-22; Heb. 1:3,13). Then God promised to make Christ's enemies His footstool. To understand this phrase, we must understand the ancient custom wherein the victor would place his foot upon the neck of the defeated foe (cf. Josh. 10:24,25). This is what Jesus did in His work of atonement on the cross. At His return, this task will be finally completed, and the faithful will be overcomers with Him (1 Cor. 15:24, 25-28; Rev. 3:21). As subjects of the King of the world, they will also be willing participants in the kingdom (110:3a; 2 Tim. 2:12). The Lord will reign supreme after having destroyed all His enemies with the authority and strength of the Almighty Lord of Hosts standing at His right side. The time of God's grace and patience, in which we are now living, would by then have been past. The time of wrath and vengeance had come (Isa. 11:4, Rev. 19:15,16).

Yet another prophetic declaration concerning the Messiah is that He is an Eternal Priest. Jesus Christ has the divine appointment of both King and Priest which was typified by Melchizedek, ("King of righteousness"; Gen. 14:18; Heb. 6:20-7:26; Zech. 6:13). He is above, interceding on our behalf. One great day, our great King/Priest shall bring in an era of peace and contentment such as the world has never known. His head shall be lifted up and exalted because of the victory He has won (110:7).

Prayer for today: *Father, thank You that You have made every provision for us in Christ Jesus to walk in victory and love this day. You have given us power and authority to tread upon serpents and scorpions and have dominion over all the power of the enemy.*

Read Psalms 111 &112 *June 3*

Key Verse: Psalm 111:10 *"The fear of the Lord is the beginning of wisdom..."*.

Psalm 111 and 112 are acrostic psalms (all sentences begin with a consecutive letter of the Hebrew alphabet) that are identical in structure. They have been called "the twin psalms". Undoubtedly they were composed by the same author, but that is unknown.

Psalm 111 is a congregational hymn of praise for God's righteous works, faithfulness and compassion. What are God's works? They are the marvelous, powerful, just, and truthful things He does to save and redeem us (111:7, 9a). The greatest was sending His Son Jesus to provide us with redemption through His blood. How has He caused His words to be remembered (111:4a)? The Holy Scriptures were written to be studied by all who love Him and take pleasure in learning more about Him (111:2). They are those people who have a healthy fear of the Lord and are the ones who exclaim: "Holy and awesome is His name" (111:9b). The psalmist affirms that this fear of the Lord is the beginning of wisdom (Prov. 1:7; 2:10; 3:13-18; 4:5-9; 8:11; James 1:5; 3:13, 17). Because they respect the Lord so much, they delight in His Law (112:1) and are prompted to study His Word more. This way they gain knowledge discernment, and a good understanding, that they may do the Lord's commands and please Him (111:10).

The Lord's holy and righteous character gives rise to His grace and compassion upon mankind. He is ever faithful to supply the needs of those who fear Him (111:4b-5), just as He is faithful to His covenant, which the psalmist illustrates by restating how God brought the children of Abraham into the Promised Land (111:6b). A major theme of the book of Psalms is that God's mercy endures forever. In this psalm we learn that in addition His righteousness, praise, and precepts will also endure forever (113:3, 10b).

Psalm 112 begins by expanding upon the closing thought of Psalm 111. The perspective of Psalm 112 is different from 111, yet there are parallels. The previous psalm emphasized the righteousness of God who is to be feared. This psalm emphasizes the righteousness of the godly man who fears the Lord.

The psalmist continues by describing the godly person's qualities. He will receive the blessings that those who are faithful to the covenant enjoy. He will prosper with enduring riches (Prov. 8:18) and have many descendants (cf. 37:25-26). He will be like a light in the darkness, for he will radiate the Lord in his life (34:5; 2 Cor.3:18; 4:6). Just as the psalmist said in the previous psalm about the Lord being "gracious and full of compassion" (111:4b), so the same is said about the righteous man at the identical point in the psalm (112:4b). The person who loves and follows the Lord will become like Him. As he daily walks with God, he will become more like His image and partake of the divine nature of God (2 Pet. 1:3-8). This must be the goal of every believer: to be more like Jesus. To accomplish this, we too must greatly delight in the Word of the Lord, and practice what it teaches (111:10; 112:1).

The godly person will be gracious and generous in both giving and lending to help the poor, since he reflects the divine character of God who enjoys giving blessings. He will be honoured and exalted, but this is not the motivation for doing so. It is because of his love for God that he can also love others. When problems come his way, he will not be afraid, since his faith is steadfast and his confidence is in the Lord.

Prayer for today: *Father, we Your children delight in Your works as we study Your Word and rejoice in Your great and precious promises. Thank You for Your perfect love that casts out all fear. We put our trust in You again this day and fear no evil, for we are sheltered in Your everlasting arms.*

Read Psalms 113, 114 &115   *June 4*

Key Verse: Psalm 115:1 *"Not unto us, O Lord, not unto us, but to Your name give glory, because of Your mercy, and because of Your truth."*

Psalms 113-118 are known as the "Hallel Psalms" (Hebrew for "praise") because the repeated exclamation of "Hallelujah", translated as "praise the Lord", is the theme of these psalms. This collection was used in the worship services on the occasions of the Hebrew feasts to express their joy and gratitude to God.

Psalm 113 begins with the invitation for the Lord's servants of every generation, from the east to the west at all times from dawn to dusk, to praise the Lord forevermore (113:2-3; Mal. 1:11). In praising His "name" (113:1-3; 115:1), we recognize the manifestations of His person and His revealed nature (Isa. 42:8; 30:27). We also are to praise Him for His incomparableness which the psalmist pictures in two ways: His transcendence and His condescension, are not set in contrast, but are complimentary. He truly "dwells on high" yet even the heavens cannot contain Him, and His ways are incomprehensible to the human mind (1 Kings 8:27; Job 26:11-14. His eminence is evident when He humbles Himself as a caring Father who sees the needs of mankind. Truly the earth is full of mercy, and at the same time the heavens are full of His glory (113:4).

The psalmist gives illustrations of God's condescension in raising up the poor and needy from the lowest depths of despair (from mourning, represented by the "ash heap"). He wipes away the tears of His children and makes them to rejoice (Rev. 21:4, Isa. 25:8; 35:10). These examples are taken from Hannah's song of praise to God for healing her barrenness (113:7-8; 1 Samuel 2:8; Luke 1:52). The psalmist uses this as yet another example of God's loving compassion (113:9). God not only intervenes to help with their conditions, but He also lifts them up and seats them with the princes of the righteous (113:8; Eph. 2:6). The greatest example of God's condescension, however, is His coming in the form of a humble man, as our Saviour Jesus Christ (Phil. 2:5-11).

With beautiful poetic imagery and in perfect Hebrew poetry, the psalmist of **Psalm 114** describes the mighty presence of God in leading the children of Israel out of Egypt. This is the greatest event in Israel's history. It pictures the miraculous events which led to His claim on Israel as His inheritance. He named Jerusalem as the place where He chose to have His sanctuary (78:54; Ex. 15:17). He parted the Red Sea at the beginning of their journey (Ex. 14:21). He dried up the Jordan River, which marked the end of their wilderness wanderings (114:3; Josh. 3:16). The hills shook and Mount Sinai trembled at the power and majesty of His presence (29:5-6; 68:8; 97:5; Ex. 19:18; Jud. 5:4; Heb. 12:18, 26). His power was also made manifest in the miracle of water pouring forth from the rock (78:15-16; Ex. 17:6; Num. 10:11). This psalm is purposely placed in the midst of the Hallel Psalms because the deliverance of God is something for which we must continually thank and praise Him.

In **Psalm 115**, the psalmist expresses the superior glory of God, and to Him alone belongs all the glory. As the psalmist stressed, the nation of Israel deserves no praise (115:1) neither do the man-made idols of the heathen. This is the main emphasis of this psalm. The heathen mock God's people by asking, "Where is your God?" Possibly the question was asked because they saw the children of Israel in distress and trouble without help from their God (cf. 42:3, 10; Joel 2:17; Isa. 36:18-20; 37:15-20). The psalmist affirms that to those who trust and fear Him, He is indeed a real help (115:9-11). However, help comes in God's own timing. Another reason they asked this question was that, because their gods were always visible, they could not fathom the God of Israel who was unseen because He is Spirit (John 1:18; 4:24).

The psalmist mocks the idols and the heathen who make and worship them. Both are vain, useless, and futile. The idol worshipper is stupid, irrational, and unreasonable (115:8; Rom. 1:23-25). How could someone make an idol himself, and then worship it? (135:15-18;

Isa. 40:18-20, 25: 44:6, 9-10; Jer. 10:1-6; Habakkuk 2:18-19). In contrast, God is truly sovereign, wise and loving. Unlike the idol, He is a true helper and a protector of His people. He is alive and active. He interacts and communicates with His people. He is the God of miracles who brings deliverance and blessing to those who fear Him. Interestingly, the three categories of Old Testament people who received blessings from God (Israel, priests, and Gentile God-fearers, 115:9-13) are now one. They are those whose faith is in the Lord Jesus Whom they love and serve. They are the true Israel (Gal. 3:26 -29; Rom. 9:6-8), the holy priesthood (1 Pet. 2:9), and those who fear God from every nation.

Prayer for today: *How wonderful it is to be called Your children, Father God! We wonder at the works of Your great power and, at the same time, stand amazed at Your loving concern and tenderness toward us. We join your servant David to give thanks to Thee, O Lord, among the peoples!*

Read Psalms 116, 117&118 June 5

Key Verse: Psalm 118:28 *"You are my God, and I will praise You; You are my God, I will exalt You."*

Although **Psalm 116** is read in the first person singular, it was most likely a song used for corporate worship in connection with the Hebrew feasts when individuals would come before the Lord at the sanctuary to pay their vows (116:14, 17-18). This included thanksgiving and praise to God for all His benefits bestowed upon them. The psalm begins with a single worshipper's expression of love to the Lord for His goodness, lovingkindness, and mercy shown in hearing and answering prayers. Since the Lord had proved Himself faithful in hearing his supplications, the worshipper resolved to call upon Him for the rest of his life (116:2).

The Lord's grace and compassion were bountiful to the grateful servant of God with his simple, child-like faith (116:6, 16). God delivered him in the fullest sense of the word. He preserved and saved his life, gave him rest (a term implying comfort, peace of heart and circumstance), brought joy to his heart, put his feet upon solid ground so that he might not stumble (116:8), and God delivered his soul from death. This is exactly what redemption through the blood of Jesus does. He has saved us from the death we deserved because of our sin, and has given us eternal life. Since God had given the worshipper of life, he knew that God was the only one in whom there was truth and in whom he could put his trust. He came to understand that it was vain to trust in men, since all men were false (116:11; 118:8; Rom.3:4).

The worshipper understands that there is nothing he can give God in return for all He has done for him (Micah 6:6-8), except to be faithful in paying his vows of offering unto Him the sacrifice of thanksgiving and praise. God's cup of salvation had been graciously offered to him, just as it is to all people. All we have to do is reach out and receive it with a humble heart of gratitude and love for God (116:13).

Although **Psalm 117** is the shortest in the psalter, with only sixteen words in the Hebrew, it is pregnant with insight and meaning, and comes in the very middle point of the Bible. It is a missionary-minded psalm which shows the purpose and plan of God that includes all people from every nation. The Gentiles are called upon to join in manifold praises to God, for they too can enjoy all His benefits (cf. Rom. 15:9-11). In the second clause, an uncommon word is used in the call to praise God; it has been translated as "laud" (NKJV), or "extol" (NIV). Actually it is implied in the meaning a joyous celebration of God with a high voice. At wedding celebrations today in the Middle East, an ancient celebration sound of a high pitched shrill sounded by women can be heard. This might be the very form of praise intended in the word. Truly, the Lord who is full of mercy and truth deserves all our praise and shouts of joy in every form possible.

Psalm 118 is a hymn of thanksgiving for the wonderful deliverance that God gave His people and as such it is a fitting conclusion to the "Hallel Psalms". Probably written in response to a battle won because God enabled His people to be strengthened, it was then adapted for congregational use. It appears to have been a processional and responsive hymn that was sung by many people as they entered the courts of the house of the Lord to worship Him (118:19-20). Since it is a celebration song, the tone is joyous.

The psalmist expresses utter confidence in God alone. When insurmountable odds were against him, he claimed the victory in the name of the Lord and received His help. The "right hand of the Lord", which represents strength and power, is praised for valiantly giving the victory. The enemies were overcome through the strength of "the stone which the builders rejected". The psalmist was likely referring to the small nation of Israel which had been despised and rejected, but with the victory in battle had become the chief power, which was "the Lord's doing" (118:23). The New Testament explains this prophetically: for the righteous, this chief cornerstone is the precious living stone chosen by God (1 Peter 2:4,5), the foundation of salvation (Acts

4:11,12) and the chief foundational stone that holds together the household of God (the Church) that it may be strong and inhabited by His Spirit (Eph.2:20-22). It can never be put to shame (1 Peter 2:6; Isa. 28:16). This stone is none other than our Lord Jesus, the Messiah, who came in the name of the Lord and who was given by God as the Light (118:26,27; John 12:13). He was rejected by His own nation, but one day all will know that He is the King who will rule on the throne of David. To those who are unrighteous and disobedient to God, however, this Stone will fall and crush them with the wrath of God (Matthew 21:42-44; 1 Peter 2:7,8; Isaiah 8:14).

Prayer for today: *Father, we present our hearts to You this day, eager to declare Your works. We proclaim with the psalmist that "You are good and Your lovingkindness is everlasting." Grant that we, Your servants, may speak Your word with all confidence and see Your hand extended to perform signs and wonders in Jesus' name.*

Read Psalm 119: 1-56   June 6

Key Verse: Psalm 119:11 *"Your Word I have hidden in my heart, that I might not sin against You."*

Psalm 119 is not only the longest chapter in the whole Bible, but is also one of the most beautiful chapters, dedicated to expressing the meaning, purpose and value of the Word of God. It is certainly the most elaborate and splendid Hebrew poem. It is a perfect acrostic, having twenty-two stanzas, one for each letter of the Hebrew alphabet. Each stanza has eight verses; each beginning with the same letter.

Amazingly, every verse, with the exception of 90 and 122, mentions the Law of God, or one of its ten synonyms. The **Law**, which is the translation of the Hebrew word Torah, is better rendered as "teaching" or "instruction". It includes the first five books of the Bible wherein is found much more than just the Law and legislation that God gave to Moses. Since the Mosaic legislation, including the ten commandments, is so very important, it came to be called the Law. **Testimonies** refers to the words of the Lord that bear witness to Him. **Precepts** are the many authoritative principles that the Lord has given for His people to obey and follow. **Statutes** are translated from the Hebrew word meaning "engrave" or "write". It also may be translated as "custom" (v.132). Statutes refers to the authoritative written word of God which was engraved upon stone as a lasting ordinance. **Commandments** refers specifically to the ten commandments. Psalm 119 teaches us that they are faithful (v.86), all-encompassing (v.96), truth (v.151), righteousness (v.172), and that they are a delight which makes one wiser (vv. 98, 143). **Judgments** of God are those divine rulings that bring justice, and are so called because God is the Judge. Since He is just and righteous, they are referred to as righteous, good, and upright which endure forever and bring help (e.g. vv. 7, 39, 62, 137, 160, 175). A similar synonym for judgments is **Ordinances** which are those divine decrees or orders that are binding upon mankind. The **Word** is the most common synonym for the Law. It refers to whatever God says. God's **Way** or **Path** are yet other synonyms, referring to all His teachings that instruct us in the way we should go.

Psalm 119 seems to be modelled after the psalm of David, 19:7-11, wherein he uses five different synonyms for the Law. King David had a tremendous love for the Word of God (1:2). If Psalm 119 was not written by him, it was authored by another righteous man who was well versed in the writings of David and who also had a deep love for the Holy Scriptures and devotion to God's instruction. Surely as the psalmist wrote these words, he felt the inspiration of the Holy Spirit of God upon him. Little did he know at the time, that his own writings would one day become a part of the Canon of Scripture, the beloved Word of God that he praised so highly.

Within this psalm, we find good food for the soul that can so easily be understood by all. It hardly needs further comment. The lengthy psalm reveals that praise to God for His Holy Word cannot be exhausted. With the exception of verses 1-3 and 115, every word is directed to the Lord in prayer. We learn by this that when we pray, we too should praise God for His Word. By His word we come to know Him. Through it, He has revealed Himself to us. Learning more of God's "righteous judgments" leads us to not only praise Him more, but to praise Him with a pure and upright heart (v.7).

It is no wonder that the psalmist begins by saying how blessed is the person who walks in the way of the Lord, and who keeps His testimonies. In doing so, that person shows evidence that seeking the Lord with his whole heart, pleases God. The more we have His Word in our hearts (which includes committing it to memory), the more we abide in Him and the greater the defense we have against sin (v.11; John 14:23; 15:7,8). In hiding God's Word in our hearts, we show that it is a very special treasure put into the most important place to serve the most important purpose; keeping us from sin (cf. Job 23:12).

How do we learn to walk in God's ways? By reading and studying His precious and Holy Word. Although the psalmist loves God's Word and practices it, he still recognizes that he has fallen short in his ability to keep the whole law of Moses (vv. 4-6; James

1:25; 2:10; Rom. 7:9-13). Only our Lord Jesus who was perfect, was able to do this. Through His strength in us, we can still please God as we grow to become more in His image (Matt. 5:48; Phil. 3:12). The psalmist was probably one of the people in his day who knew the Word of God best. Still he humbly expresses that he has more to learn and more to understand concerning God's precepts (v. 27). He prays, "open my eyes, that I may see wondrous things from Your Law" (v. 18). This should be the prayer of everyone who reads the Bible. Through the Holy Spirit we can truly be enlightened in our understanding and knowledge of God.

Prayer for today: *Open our eyes, Lord, that we may indeed see wondrous things from Your Word this day. Incline our hearts to what You are saying and establish Your Word in us, that we "might not sin against You," but rather honour and please you.*

Read Psalm 119: 57-120

Key Verse: Psalm 119:105 *"Your word is a lamp to my feet and a light to my path."*

The psalmist uses may beautiful expressions to describe the wonderful things the Word of God does for him. The same is true for all believers who love and devote themselves to reading it and who have hidden it in their hearts. Throughout the psalm we learn that the Word cleanses our way, causes us to rejoice, brings delight and counsel, revives, teaches, strengthens and gives us life, hope, comfort, songs, wisdom, understanding and great peace. It is a light and a lamp to our feet that we may see clearly the right path that we should follow. The Word of God directs our steps. What marvelous benefits the Lord gives through His Word!

Because of the poet's attempt to start every verse with the same letter of the Hebrew letter within each stanza, it has caused little continuity of thought throughout. Although the theme of the wonderful Word of God remains the same, the thoughts within each stanza are often unrelated. In many stanzas the same thoughts are repeated, but expressed in different ways. This is not a vain repetition. Such an important topic deserves to be emphasized in order to ensure that it may be understood and become real to the readers.

If the psalmist were not David, he may have been a Levite who continually studied and copied the Law, like a scribe as was Ezra. The Levites received no inheritance of land, for the Lord Himself was their inheritance. The psalmist relates to this when he says, "You are my portion, O Lord" (v. 57). He has laid a personal claim on God's Law, which is part of his inheritance (v. 56, 111). He finds everything He needs in God. He is content and not tempted to be covetous or envious of the possessions of others.

The psalmist may have been the "young man" who learned that by living according to God's Word, his way was cleansed (v.9). Even though he was young, he claimed to have greater spiritual understanding than his teachers and even more than the ancient sages. The reason is because he constantly read, meditated upon, and obeyed God's Word. He prayed for understanding and he was spiritually enlightened (vv. 99-100, 18, 33-34).

The psalmist recognized that when he had been afflicted, it was the Lord's chastisement upon him to bring him back to the right path. In this divine form of discipline, he acknowledges that God was good and the affliction was also good. As a result he drew closer to God, learned more about God and His Word, and it brought him back to the straight and narrow way (67-68, 71; Hebrews 12:5-12). Because he delighted in the Word and was familiar with it, when he was afflicted it did not lead to his fall or his death (v. 92). He knew he could claim the promises and blessings of God which are found in His Word. He knew he could call out to a merciful God who hears his prayers. As a result of his knowledge of God's Word, he had the faith that God would revive him, as well as accept his "freewill offerings" of praise and thanksgiving (v. 108).

Another predominant topic within this psalm is the contrast between the righteous and the wicked. The righteous shall be safe and preserved, but the wicked evildoers who do not obey the Word of God will be rejected and cast away (vv. 117-119). Although the wicked (proud) have bound him with cords, dug pits for him, laid snares for him, slandered and wronged him with lies, persecuted him without reason, and almost killed him (vv. 61, 69, 78, 85-87, 95, 110), they were not able to overcome him because he continued to meditate on God's Word (v.78). He kept true to the Lord by not forgetting, forsaking, or straying from His laws and precepts (v. 61, 87, 110). The Lord was his hiding place and his shield, just as He will be for us in our time of need. In God's Word we have the assurance that He will uphold His children.

Prayer for today: *Father, Your Word is truth and has given us great assurance in a seemingly hopeless world. We ask for an ever-increasing desire to read, meditate upon, and memorize Your precious Words of life which light our Christian walk.*

It not only grieves, but it angers the psalmist to see many who do not follow the Lord's Law. He knows that if they do not obey they will not see the salvation of the Lord. He is full of zeal to preach and teach others so that they too would love God, follow His Word, and not perish (vv.136, 139, 150, 155, 158). The psalmist, had become disgusted with those who persisted in wickedness and stubbornly refused to follow God's ways. He describes them as oppressors, enemies, persecutors, and princes (rich tyrants) who were wicked, proud and treacherous. Because of their unbridled wickedness and their total disregard for God's Word, the psalmist desires to see only righteousness, and he calls upon God to intervene, saying, "It is time for You to act, O Lord" (v.126). This is not only a cry for judgment upon the wicked, but it is in effect a call for God to send the much needed Messiah into the sinful world. Only the Messiah could ever bring a change to these sinful people, and only He would one day bring in a era of righteousness upon the earth. When God sent Jesus into the world, that was the specific time, in the fullness of time, that God had chosen to act in history. Salvation and redemption could come to mankind. Jesus was "God's salvation" that the psalmist longed for (v. 166), just as He was for the aged Simeon who exclaimed, "For my eyes have seen Your salvation" (Luke 2:30).

The psalmist is so very sincere and it is his great love for God that causes him to follow the Law in the best way he can. He admits he had gone astray, like a lost sheep. Since He is God's sheep, the Lord will indeed seek him out, find him, and restore him to the fold (v.176). He has purposed in his heart to have all his steps directed by God's Word. It was not possible for sin to have dominion over him (v.133; Rom. 6:11-14). He might slip, but he would not stay down.

The psalmist did not try to figure out the meaning of the Torah with his own intellect. He constantly prayed for God to give him the understanding, and he acknowledged that truly the Lord did give him enlightenment and understanding (v. 130). The Holy Spirit unveils wonderful truths that give light in the darkness and cause one to truly live and have that "great peace" that the psalmist found (v. 144, 165; Rom. 8:6, 11). He gives spiritual discernment and causes us to have the mind of Christ (1 Cor. 2:12-16).

As an Old Testament person, the psalmist lived under the Law. Because of his deep desire to know God and the true essence of His

Word (the spirit of the law, and not the letter of the law), he was in actuality led by the Spirit, and as such he was not literally under the law (Gal. 5:18; Rom. 7:6; 8:14). It was people such as himself, who loved God, longed for His salvation, were led by the Spirit, and had a passion for his Word (not from a head knowledge) who would have recognized Jesus as the Messiah when He came into the world, as did Simeon. Sadly, people of this type were very few. Even the Pharisees and Sadducees who prided themselves in their knowledge of the Law, did not recognize Jesus as the promised Messiah.

The Word of God leads us into all truth, so let us determine, as did the psalmist, to cherish the Bible, study it, and follow it. Truly the Word of God is rightly described in Psalm 119 as good, right, perfection, sweet, wonderful, righteous, upright, faithful, truth, a delight, and everlasting. Since God Himself is the author, and He is all these things, so is His Word.

Prayer for today: *Father, as we receive Your Word today and cherish it in our hearts, we expect Your truth to pierce our innermost beings, revealing the thoughts and intentions of our hearts, which may be pleasing or displeasing to You. Thank You, again, for Your Words which are living and active, sharper than any two-edged sword, and able to separate us from any evil and draw us unto You.*

Read Psalms 120-124   *June 9*

Key Verse: *Psalm 121: 1,2 "I will lift up my eyes to the hills — from whence comes my help? My help comes from the Lord..."*

Psalms 120 to 134 form a collection called the "Songs of Ascent". This likely refers to the pilgrimage of worshippers who have to ascend in order to get to Jerusalem. The city is topographically higher than the surrounding land. These songs may have been sung as the pilgrims went up to Jerusalem on the joyous occasions of the great feasts when they went to worship in the House of the Lord.

The writer of **Psalm 120** is greatly distressed because his neighbours showed him animosity. Unlike his adversaries, who were violent and loved war (metaphorically described as the barbaric people of Meshech and Kedar), he was a man of peace, therefore he did not take vengeance against them, though they maliciously slandered him. He went to the Lord in prayer. His past experiences of God's faithfulness strengthened the faith that God would again save him, and indeed God heard him. Since the enemies' lying lips and false tongues were like sharp fiery arrows that hit him, they deserved to be shot with equally sharp arrows, and to suffer upon burning hot coals (cf. Jer. 9:3, 8; Prov. 26: 18,19; James 3:6). Significantly, we learn from the New Testament that this type of lying people will indeed suffer upon burning coals, for they shall go to the lake of fire (Rev. 21:8).

Psalm 121 teaches us that our loving God is interested in us and He continually watches over us and cares for us. The psalmist's face is toward Jerusalem, which is in the hill country. He looks up with faith and expectancy toward the Holy City of God. In the Lord's House is the presence of the Almighty God. He who created the universe, condescended to be near His people and to be their source of help (119:151). God watches over His people, not only collectively, but individually. He is a personal God (33:13-14; 2 Chron. 16:9; Prov. 15:3; Heb. 4:13). Unlike the unanswering Baal whom Elijah taunted about sleeping (1 Kings 18:27), our God never sleeps. He is ever watchful to protect us from harm (e.g. Jonah 4:6). He is the One who preserves us, physically and spiritually, at all times, wherever we are, even into eternity (cf. Gen. 28:15).

Psalm 122 may have been the song the joyous pilgrims sang after they had entered the gates of Jerusalem. As such, it serves as a sequel to the previous two songs of ascent. Those who came to worship God, from all the tribes or families, were so glad to congregate together in unity for the purpose of giving thanks to the Lord. We, likewise should count it a joy and a privilege to have fellowship in God's House with other believers. One of the things for which the worshippers thanked God was the righteous and just rule of their king (possibly David himself or one of his descendants who, like David, did what was right in the sight of the Lord). Their desire was to see the continuance of worship to the Lord at His Holy House which would be possible only if Jerusalem was secure, prosperous, and peaceful. Therefore, they resolved to pray for the peace of Jerusalem. This ultimately means to pray for Jerusalem to see the true peace of God that is found only in His Son Jesus, the Prince of Peace, who will come as the King of the world, to rule and reign from His Holy City, the New Jerusalem.

In the previous psalm, the pilgrims lifted up their eyes to the House of the Lord. Now, in **Psalm 123**, they lift up their eyes to the Lord Himself, for only He can deliver them from their distress. The look of the eye can often communicate better than words. We are to be the Lord's submissive servants, always watching our Master that we may do His bidding for His pleasure. Just as the servant waits patiently to receive favour from his master, so we can look to God for mercy, and our Master knows our every need.

Psalm 124 beautifully describes God's deliverance, expressing that if God is for us, who can be against us (Rom. 8:31)? If it had not been that the Lord was on their side, the pilgrims' destruction would be certain. God rescued them, just in the nick of time, before the flood waters of death overcame them. In gratitude and confidence in Him, the rescued pilgrims express their thanks by blessing the Lord, who has not only given them life, but who has given them justice, mercy, and new-found freedom to enjoy life, like a bird released from captivity (cf. 91:3). Through Jesus Christ, we too have been made free indeed! (John 8:36; Gal. 5:1).

Prayer for today: *Lord God, we lift up our eyes to You today and every day for help and protection. You are our Keeper, the Maker of heaven and earth who never sleeps or slumbers. We put our faith and trust in You to protect us from all evil. Thank You for the freedom from fear we have as we rest in Your perfect love.*

Read Psalms 125-129 *June 10*

Key Verse: Psalm 128:1 *"Blessed is every one who fears the Lord, who walks in His ways."*

Jerusalem is on a hill surrounded by many other hills which serve to help in its fortification. In **Psalm 125** we see a graphic picture of our Lord standing firm and strong, like a mountain range, surrounding His people with continuous, stable protection that gives peace (cf. Isa. 54:10; Phil.4:7). Those who put their trust in Him, He will cause to stand firm and strong forever. He especially protects Mount Zion since He has laid claim to it as His own (cf. Heb. 12:22; Joel 3;17,18). Such beautiful imagery expresses the fact that our eternal, undying souls will always be surrounded by the Lord, even in the heavenlies. While we remain in our earthly bodies, however, we can expect trials and tribulations, but "the scepter of wickedness shall not rest". It shall not remain on us forever. The Lord will not send trials our way that we cannot overcome, "lest the righteous cannot bear it and fall into sin" (125:3; 1 Cor. 10:13). In contrast, those who in times of turmoil were weak and succumbed to temptation, so that they turned away to walk (continuously) along the crooked paths, would not remain. They would be led away, like a suffering captive. Indeed those who live in sin, are like prisoners condemned to death.

Psalm 126 refers to the joyous return to Zion of the remnant from the Exile in Babylon. When the answer to their prayers came, it seemed to good to be true, like a dream come true. This is the reaction that the decree of Cyrus must have brought to the exiles (Ezra 1:1-4). All the Gentiles could see clearly that it was their God who had done this great thing for them. As a result, the Lord received the glory not from only His people, but even from the heathen. Those who returned prayed that even more of their people would pour back to Zion, in the manner of the dry river beds of the south, in the Negev of Israel that suddenly overflow with rushing water during the short rainy season. These are the faithful ones who wept with a burden for lost souls in the distant harvest fields. They will not return empty handed, without fruit for their labour. There will be a harvest of lost souls brought to the Lord while in distant harvest fields.

Psalm 127 clearly emphasizes the futility and folly of human effort without help from God. In every area of our life, personal, social, or civil, we need to depend upon the Lord to succeed according to divine standards. Even the building of a home for one's family is in vain if the Lord's blessing is not upon it. It must be built upon the Rock (Matt. 7:24,25; Prov. 24:3). In one's work, it is vain to wake up early to only worry and work hard until the point of exhaustion, and then return home to only worry some more and be envious of what others have. Those who trust in God to provide all their needs, however, do not need to worry, and God gives them a peaceful sleep which results from their peace of mind (cf. Mark 4:26, 27; Prov. 10:22). They have a much healthier and rewarding life. They are rewarded by God with children who are a great source of joy and who will become a source of strength to their aged parents. These children will bring them honour, for they will be well respected at the gate (the place where civil affairs were conducted).

Psalm 128 continues with the same thoughts that ended Psalm 127. It teaches that the basis of a truly happy and successful home is the fear of the Lord. Those who obey, love and reverence the Lord, following the principles for living laid down in the Holy Bible, will be blessed by the Lord with provisions. For the ancients, the greatest blessing was to have many children (Deut. 28:1-4). They ensured that the parents would be well cared for all their days, and that the family name would be carried on and increase. Godly families are the foundation of a healthy and prosperous society.

In **Psalm 129**, the writer recalls the past afflictions of Israel since the early stages of the nation's existence. In so doing, he is given confidence to realize that God did not allow the enemies to prevail. For a time the "plowers" did their job of persecution and tearing up the ground, but God turned it for good, for where there were deep furrows, God gave them growth, like a good crop. In contrast to the flourishing of God's people (Zion, the Church of Jesus Christ), the wicked who hate the righteous are likened to the grass that grows on the roofs of Middle Eastern houses; they may take root and begin to grow, but they are weak because they are planted in bad ground and soon they wither and die (cf. Matt. 13:3-9).

Prayer for today: *Thank You, dear Lord, for the growth You produce in our lives. Though Your planting and pruning may seem harsh to us, we know You mean it for our good. When we walk in Your ways, we cannot help but be blessed! May we also be a blessing to others.*

Read Psalms 130-134   June 11

Key Verse: Psalm 134:1 *"Behold, bless the Lord, all you servants of the Lord..."*

In **Psalm 130**, the psalmist utters a reverent, penitential prayer wherein he ascends from out of the depths of despair and misery to the heights of hope with dependence upon God's mercy and redemption. He recognizes that he is a sinner who could never hope to stand before God unless his sins be forgiven. His knowledge that God is a forgiving God, full of mercy and compassion, gives him hope and causes him to greatly fear the Lord (cf. 103:8-13; Lam. 3:21-23; Neh. 9:17; 1 Pet. 1:17). The psalmist waits patiently, expectantly and anxiously, trusting with faith in the promises of God's Word that He will forgive and restore. As the coming of the morning light, the darkness is gone when God looks upon the penitent with favour (cf. 37:5-7). His personal experience with God's mercy caused him to preach to all Israel. He challenged them to hope in the Lord so that they too might come to know His inner peace, for "with Him is abundant redemption" (130:7). Indeed, God did provide wonderful redemption from sin for all those who have put their faith in Jesus Christ.

Psalm 131 is a beautiful expression of humility and trust in the Lord. David does not consider himself great in his own eyes, nor does he profess to be a wise scholar (Rom. 12:3, 16; Prov. 16:18; James 4:6, 10). In fact, he admits his own limitations. He has come to the point where he does not have to depend on the things of this world for his contentment, just like a weaned child no longer has to depend upon being nursed by his mother to receive comfort and contentment (Eph. 4:14; Heb. 5: 12-14). David, therefore has grown spiritually. He finds contentment in the Lord. Because of his inner peace he longs for others to have the same. Therefore he calls upon Israel to hope in the Lord. All believers in Jesus (spiritual Israel) need to likewise continually grow in their faith and become detached from the temporal things of this world.

Psalm 132 commemorates the bringing of the Ark of the Covenant into Jerusalem by David. It reiterates God's promise concerning the eternal establishment of the throne of David. David sought to honour the Lord by finding a suitable place for the Ark. The Ark symbolized the presence of the Almighty God. After the Philistines returned the captured Ark, it rested in Kirjath Jearim, meaning "town of the woods" (1 Sam. 6:21-7:1,2). The pilgrim singers may have re-enacted the event when David, from Bethlehem Ephrathah, went to find the Ark in the woods. With great rejoicing he took it to Jerusalem to worship God at His tabernacle. The resting place of His sacred Ark is called God's footstool and strength (132:6-8). Along with the prayer for a permanent Tabernacle for the Ark, the pilgrims prayed that it would be accompanied by a righteous priesthood (132:9). When the Ark had been captured, there had been a corrupted priesthood (1 Sam. 2:12-17,22). A second prayer request was that the Lord would fulfill His promise to David concerning an everlasting dynasty (132:10-12; cf. 2 Sam.7). The Lord answered prophetically that He would indeed dwell in Zion, in His Temple (John 1:14; 2 Cor. 6:16; Heb. 9:11). He would have a righteous and saved priesthood (all believers in Jesus; 1 Pet. 2:5, 9), and that David's line would not be cut off, but grow strong ("horn of salvation", Luke 1:69) and have a "lamp" (glory revealed; 1 Kings 11:36). Jesus was that prepared and promised Lamp, the Light of the world who revealed God's glory (132: 13-18).

Psalm 133 praises unity and brotherly harmony. Jesus Christ had prayed that His followers would be one, which not only brings glory to God, but which testifies of the truth to the world that God sent Him (John 17:20-22). Unity comes from the bond of love which is evidenced by sacrificially serving and admonishing others (Col. 3:14-16; Eph. 4:1-6). King David illustrates the pleasantness of unity in two ways. It is like the special abundant, precious oil of consecration that was poured over Aaron when he was dedicated as high priest (Ex. 29:7-9; 40:13-16; Lev. 8:12). It flowed down his face onto his priestly garments, over the breastplate upon which were the names of the twelve tribes of Israel. When unity spreads, it will have an influence on all the people, which is pleasing in the sight of the Lord. It shows their consecration to God. A second illustration is that brotherly harmony and unity among the people of God is like the fall of abundant dew on them. This is found on Mount Hermon. Unity gives rise to fertility, growth, and revival. In the seasons when there is no rain in

Israel, the dew is essential for the fertility of the ground (cf. Haggai 1:10-11), just as unity is essential for believers that they may be fruitful for the Lord.

Psalm 134 is an appropriate conclusion for the songs of ascent, which was most likely sung as the benediction at the close of the evening worship. It may have been the final song of the pilgrims before they left for their respective towns. The psalm begins by addressing the Levitical priests and watchmen who stand in the House of the Lord throughout the night. Their job was not merely to be guards or gatekeepers, but to be worshippers as well (1 Chron. 9:26-27, 33). On a rotating basis, there were always Levites continually standing before the Lord to minister (cf. Deut. 10:8; 1 Chron. 23:30) with uplifted hands representing their pure hearts lifted up to God in praise and worship (28:2; 141:2). This exhortation, however, is applicable to all servants (priests) of the Lord in every generation to continually bless the Lord and be faithful in carrying out their sacred duties. The priests whose primary duty is to bless the Lord, then turn to bless the worshippers of the Lord before they left the sanctuary after the evening time of worship.

Prayer for today: *Thank You, Father, for the blessings You have promised Your children who dwell together in unity. We remember also Your new commandment: "love one another as I have loved you". We purpose by Your grace to walk in that most precious divine love, which You have poured into our hearts through Your Holy Spirit (Romans 5:5b).*

Read Psalms 135 & 136 *June 12*

Key Verse: Psalm 136:1 *"Oh, give thanks to the Lord, for He is good! For His mercy endures forever."*

Psalm 135 was compiled by using many different portions from other psalms and other Old Testament writings. It was undoubtedly composed for us in the Temple worship. The servants of the Lord, identified as: the priests, Levites, all the children of Israel, the Gentile God-fearers and all inhabitants of Jerusalem (135:19-21), are called upon to praise and bless the Lord. Several reasons are given as to why God's people should praise Him, with the emphasis upon God's sovereign power in nature (135:6,7) and history (135:8-12). The first reason to praise and thank Him is because "the Lord is good" (135:3; 136:1). If we were to enumerate the goodness of God we would never finish. Each individual worshipper must interpret for himself what the goodness of God means to him.

The whole psalm illustrates God's goodness and gives reasons why the people of the Lord are to praise Him. Firstly, because He had chosen them as His own special treasure (Deut. 7:6-8). What a privilege it is to be the elect of God! With it come many responsibilities. Believers today, who are God's elect, have the responsibility, as did the ancient Israelites, to be lights shining in a dark world to show others the way they should go.

With a firm and unshakable belief, the psalmist affirms that "the Lord is great" and because of His greatness He is worthy to be praised. He is the sole sovereign over the world, above all the false gods who are but the work of foolish man's hands (135:5, 15-18; 115:4-8; 95:3; 96:4,5; Deut. 10:17). The special revelation of God clearly shows His sovereignty over the world. The ultimate control over the world and the affairs of mankind is the will of God. The Israelites were to praise God for delivering them from bondage in Egypt. Believers today need to praise God for delivering them from being enslaved to sin and suffering. We, like the Israelites, must also praise God for giving us the victory over the enemy Satan, and for giving us an eternal inheritance (135:12). God is also to be praised for His righteous judgment and the compassion He shows to His people (Deut. 32:36; e.g. God's treatment of Israel during the period of the judges). Today we must bless the Lord with equal enthusiasm for He is the same yesterday, today, and forever!

Psalm 136, although different in form, is an expansion of Psalm 135 and the two are closely related in subject matter. The former is a psalm of praise; the latter of thanksgiving. Psalm 136 is clearly a responsive hymn. The first line of each verse expresses God's mercy, likely sung by the priest or Levitical song leader. The second line is the refrain which is the response of the congregation or choir: "For His mercy endures forever".

The psalm begins by describing God as good, the God of gods, and Lord of lords (Deut. 10:17). Since He is the only God, He alone has creative and miracle-working powers (136:4; 72:18). Since He is the supreme Lord, he has subjected all nations and kings under Him. This was evident when He delivered Israel from Egypt and overthrew the Pharoah. In His mercy and faithfulness, God guided them in the wilderness, gave them the Promised Land, and rescued them over and over again. He not only sustains and preserves them, but He, in His mercy, provides food for all people and creatures (104:27, 28; 145:15,16). It is no wonder the psalmist repeats 26 times that God's mercy endures forever and concludes by calling upon all flesh to "give thanks to the God of heaven" (136:26).

Prayer for today: *We give You praise and thanksgiving this day, dear Father. Your goodness and lovingkindness are boundless! Your goodness was evident in your dealings with the children of Israel as You brought them out of slavery in Egypt, and Your goodness is even more evident today as we look to Jesus, Your beloved Son whom You gave to redeem us.*

Read Psalms 137, 138&139   *June 13*

Key Verse: Psalm 139:23,24 *"Search me, O God, and know my heart...and see if there is any wicked way in me, and lead me in the way everlasting."*

In **Psalm 137** we hear of the lament of some of the Levitical musicians who went away into captivity. It is very sad at the beginning as they reflect on their past, but suddenly the tone changes and it becomes very upsetting in the end as the captives talk of the future revenge they desire on their captors. In their exile, they mourned and wept at the destruction of the Temple, the Holy City, and their own misfortunes. Their captors ridiculed them, asking them to sing, but they would rather lose their ability to play, than to play the songs in the foreign land that once belonged to the Lord's House. They would rather be paralyzed with the loss of their right hand than to forget Jerusalem, the centre of worship to God where they had once joyously played and sung.

Suddenly, their tears of sorrow changed to great anger and words of cursing for their oppressors that do not reflect the principles of the New Testament but which purport "an eye for an eye". They vented their fury against Edom who were their brothers, (descendants from Esau), who had helped and supported Nebuchadnezzar's destruction of Jerusalem (Amos 1:11; Ezek. 25:12-14). They prayed in bitterness that God would do the same to Babylon, as they had done to them and their babies. Yet such an imprecation can never be justified. They did not have the love and forgiveness of God in their hearts.

In **Psalm 138**, David expresses his resolve to boldly praise the Lord. He praises God before all the kings of the earth, and before all their gods, so that all will be ashamed of themselves and their idolatry when they hear him sing praises toward God's Holy Temple and when they hear the words of the Lord. He envisions all the heathen kings joining him in singing praises to the One and only true God. This was not fulfilled during his reign, but will be during the Messianic reign of Jesus. It will be the great glory of the Lord which will cause them to worship Him. God's glory is especially revealed in His condescension to revive, stretch out His hand, and save wretched mankind. Because of His truth and lovingkindness we are to praise Him because we can be confident that He will fulfill His purpose in our lives. He is glorified in His concern to complete "that good work in us...until the day of Jesus Christ" (Phil. 1:6; 138:8).

Psalm 139 is one of the most profound psalms. It deals with many aspects of theology and God's relationship to man. David is awestruck by God's omniscience (all-knowing) and admits that his own knowledge is limited, for man can never fully comprehend God. However, with the divine revelation in this psalm, God gave new and revolutionary understanding about Himself to David's generation and each successive one, that we also might learn more about our wonderful Lord. The psalmist is convinced that God knows everything about him. God even knows his inner most thoughts before he utters a word. Truly God looks upon the heart and knows the motivation behind all our words and deeds (139: 1-6; Heb. 4:13).

Yet another attribute of God that causes the psalmist to be awestruck, is His omnipresence (all-present). In every place upon the earth, under the earth, or above the earth, God is there. He is before us, in front of us, underneath us, above us, and around us. His divine all-seeing eyes are ever watchful for mankind (Amos 9:2). He is near so that people may find Him and experience His salvation (Act 17:27-28). Wherever His children are, even in the remotest or darkest of places, we can be sure that He is with us to guide us when we call upon Him. The brilliant light that radiates from God's presence casts out all darkness.

Yet another marvel that the psalmist expresses is God's omnipresence, omniscience (including His foreknowledge) and omnipotence (all-powerful) which are evident in the formation of the unborn child within the womb. The psalmist is aware that God knew him even before he was born; in fact He knew him from the moment of conception. God was there with him in the dark and secret place, and God was the power and infinite wisdom behind His formation and growth. How precious is the unborn child in God's sight that He would be so watchful and caring over that undying soul, and that He would have a pre-ordained plan and purpose for each new life that is conceived. The psalmist's mind has been illuminated by God's Spirit, and yet he stands in awe at the incomprehensible nature of God's thoughts which are innumerable and so very precious to him.

Reflecting upon the power and marvelous deeds of the Lord, causes the psalmist's righteous indignation to rise against the wicked sinful people of the world who speak against God to mock and curse Him. He who only magnifies and praises God wants nothing to do with such people. He wants to see divine wrath consume them so that upon the earth there will only be those who love and praise God. One day, this will come, but it will be in the Lord's perfect timing and plan. As David began the psalm, he now concludes with a similar prayer request, (that should be prayed by all believers) for God to test, search out, and probe our hearts so that all impurity will be gone. The end result of God's cleansing will be everlasting life.

Prayer for today: *Father, we join our hearts together with David in praying, "Search me, O God, and know my heart; try me and know my anxious thoughts; and see if there be any wicked way in me, and lead me in the way everlasting." (Psalm 139:23, 24).*

Read Psalms 140, 141 &142   *June 14*

Key Verse: Psalm 140:13 *"Surely the righteous shall give thanks to Your name; the upright shall dwell in Your presence."*

Psalms 140 to 143 form a distinct group because of their many similarities. They are all psalms of David when he was under difficult circumstances and internal persecution by a strong foe, but he turns to the Lord for protection and deliverance. Just as Satan schemes to cause God's people to stumble in their walk of faith, so it was with David's enemies as we see in **Psalm 140**. It was mainly because of his righteousness, inner peace, and high standards that they gathered together to wage war against him in an organized and premeditated campaign. The plotted against him, slandered, and set traps that he might fall. He prayed that God would deliver, preserve, and keep him from these violent men who sought his destruction.

When Satan and his co-workers attack us, we, like David, can be confident that God will protect us where we are most vulnerable. Like the strongest helmet, God protected David's head when the battle raged against him. As for the heads of the wicked, David prayed that their own evil would fall upon them (140:9; 141:10). If they were the victors it would reflect badly on the cause of righteousness. Therefore, for the Lord's sake, David prayed that He bring just retribution so they will not be exalted, but rather overthrown. David ends the psalm with confidence, for unlike the wicked who are cast out, he and other upright people will be defended by God and will live to thank Him since they shall have the greatest privilege — to dwell in God's presence.

In **Psalm 141**, David is in a similar circumstance as in the previous psalm, but here he is more concerned that in his suffering he not succumb to temptation. For this he asks for God's help and for reproof and correction from the righteous. He asks that his prayer and his supplication with uplifted hands be as acceptable to God and as effective as the evening offering of incense and sacrifice in the House of the Lord.

The evildoers were seeking David's downfall by tempting him to do evil like themselves, and to join in with their wicked pleasures, but David asks the Lord for strength to guard his mouth and heart from doing evil and participating in worldly pleasure and luxuries. Often the enemy attacks under the guise of friendliness which can be more effective than direct assaults. David recognizes the dangers of compromise and so he prays that he would always welcome the rebukes of the righteous if he ever starts to go off course. A loving reproof is a great kindness to a fellow believer, so he will not yield to temptation and fall into sin. It is like a soothing and pleasant oil upon one's head that is beneficial and for the receiver's own good. It is also a means whereby God helps His children to "escape safely" from the snares and traps of the workers of iniquity (141:10).

As we learn from the title of **Psalm 142**, it is a prayer of David "when he was in the cave". This likely refers to the time when he was in the cave of Adullam after fleeing from the Philistines in Gath (1 Sam. 22:1). From David's plea we can see that he had reached the depths of loneliness and despair. He cried out to God, pouring out his complaints and declaring his trouble. He may have been alone, but if his young companions were still with him (1 Sam. 21:2), he nonetheless felt alone and forsaken. God was his only Refuge. He found no refuge in Gath (1 Sam. 21:10-15). Without God, even hiding in the cave could give him no protection. God was his only portion or inheritance, for Saul had forced him to flee from his home and had likely confiscated the land of his inheritance.

David, however, had a great source of strength — his faith in God. The many snares that his strong enemies had laid against him would not prevail (142:3b; 141:9,10; 140:5). He felt secure in the Lord. God would never let him fall prey to his hunters. He felt imprisoned in the cave since Saul had taken away his freedom, yet he was confident that God would bless him abundantly and surround him with the righteous for which he would give glory to God. As history records, God did indeed surround David with many others to support and strengthen him. While hiding in that very cave, God sent four hundred men (1 Sam. 22:2) to him.

Prayer for today: *Father, You have said in Your Word that the upright shall dwell in Your presence. We thank You for making Jesus our righteousness, providing that new and living way for us to come near to You. When our hearts seem overwhelmed, we will remember that we can call upon You for strength and protection with great assurance.*

Read Psalms 143 &144   June 15

Key Verse: Psalm 144:15 *"...Happy are the people whose God is the Lord!"*

Like the previous three psalms, **Psalm 143** is composed by David. Again he complains of bitter persecution from his enemies and entreats God to hear his prayer because of His faithfulness and righteousness. The God of the covenant will keep His promises about blessing the faithful. David pleads that He will not enter into judgment of him, for because of his sin, he could never hope to be justified before God, nor could anyone else. Today, however, those who have peace with God through faith in Jesus Christ have been justified and can stand before God with the righteousness of Jesus (Rom. 3:21-26; 5:1,2; Gal. 2:16).

David feels crushed by the enemy. The persecution has caused him to be full of gloom and distress as if he had already gone down in darkness to the pit. However, when he remembers, meditates, and considers the past goodness and mighty deeds of God, he realizes that he needs some of that divine power in his life to help at such a crucial point. He is given the courage to ask God for His mercy to be delivered and revived. To quench his thirsty soul, he reaches out to God and affirms his trust in Him. David's expressions show the urgency and his great need for God and for God's guidance in his life. With a beautiful and exemplary prayer he prays, "teach me to do Your will"; a prayer we all must make if God is truly our Lord, and if we, like David, desire spiritual revival and to walk in the land of uprightness (143:10).

Psalm 144 is a psalm of David that appears to be a compilation of previous works (e.g. Psalm 18). David begins by blessing the Lord for His past blessings to him and for what He is to him. God is expressed in several metaphors that show Him to be David's Strength and Protector. In contrast to God's greatness, man is small, transitory, and insignificant (144:3,4; 8:4; 39:11; 102:11; 109:23). Even so, God is concerned about us. David understood that God can be called upon to intervene and come to our aid, "Bow down Your heavens, O Lord,

145

and come down" (144:5). The greatest example of God's coming down was with the incarnation of Jesus Christ when truly the heavenly and earthly met together in the most wonderful and unique way.

David asked for the manifestations of God's power in rescuing him from the enemy who are guilty of slandering and breaking their oaths of allegiance to him (144:8). Once delivered, David promises to create a new song in God's honour and to play upon his harp and sing His praises and offer thanksgiving. With God's complete salvation, David envisions the consequences of an ideal society that is blessed by the Lord. His sons are strong and virile, his daughters are stately and beautiful, his barns full, his cattle productive, and his city strong and peaceful. In such a state the people are happy and enjoy their material blessing. The reason for their happiness is that they are spiritually blessed since God is their Lord.

Prayer for today: *God, today we pray from our heart the prayer that David prayed, "Teach me the way in which I should walk; for to You do I lift up my soul...Teach me to do Your will, for You are my God. Let Your good Spirit lead me on level ground for the sake of Your name, O Lord..." (Psalm 143:8b-11).*

Read Psalms 145 &146   *June 16*

Key Verse: Psalm 145:3 *"Great is the Lord, and greatly to be praised..."*.

Psalm 145 is an acrostic poem that serves as an introduction to the final section of the psalter which is called the Hallelujah psalms (146-150). The theme of Psalm 145 is found in verse three (key verse). All the praises that the psalmist offers to God are because of His greatness. Although David rightly expresses that the totality of God's greatness is unsearchable (Rom. 11:33), he does a wonderful job in searching it out and illustrating it. His remarkable insight, of course, came with the help of the Holy Spirit's inspiration.

God's greatness is to be greatly praised, which David does in every way possible. He desires his praises to God to be exemplary so that others may hear them and join him. He extols, blesses, meditates, declares, speaks, utters, talks, and every day makes known with his mouth the praises of the Lord (145:1,2,5,6,7,11,12,21). Who is more fitted to do so than the king whom the Great King had appointed as leader under Him? Praising the King of kings includes telling others of His mighty acts which have been personally experienced or which were experienced by others. David's generation made an effort to tell God's mighty deeds on behalf of the nation to the next generation.

This was done through memory (oral transmission) and through singing songs (145:4,7).

The greatness of God is further illustrated in His wonderful attributes of grace, compassion, slow to anger (long-suffering), and mercy (145:8). God is good and shows general grace to all His creation. Indeed, God sends the rain on the just and the unjust alike and all His creation depends on Him for life and only in Him can there be ultimate satisfaction (145:9, 15-16; Matt. 5:45). The created realm praises the Lord and the saints of God both praise and bless Him. To do this they must talk of His glory and power to all mankind, including the glories of His everlasting Kingdom (145:13).

When those who love and fear God cry out to Him, He will certainly be near and He will hear, save, and preserve them. In these very gracious and righteous works of God, His greatness is once again evident. Another righteous way of the Lord, however, is in bringing just punishment upon the wicked. God cannot tolerate evil. At the appointed time, He will abolish evil from the face of the earth and then all flesh will perform the duty for which they were created, namely to "bless His holy name forever and ever" (145:21).

The last five psalms of the psalter from a small collection called the "Hallelujah Psalms". Since they are dedicated to praising the Lord, they all begin and end with the exclamation of "Hallelujah" (Praise Yahweh"). This is a wonderful and joyful note upon which to end the Book of Psalms. Although they are all similar, each one has a different emphasis.

In **Psalm 146**, the writer calls upon the congregation to praise the Lord and to show that he practices what he preaches. He vows that as long as he has breath, he will praise the Lord. He speaks from personal experience when he warns the people not to trust in princes (or noblemen, a term commonly used of rich and powerful men), nor in any human being for help since they cannot be reliable. At any time a person could die, for life is so fragile. But the Lord "Who keeps truth forever" is eternal and all-powerful. Upon Him we can depend, and the one whose hope is in Him is happy. God never lets us down. He is called the "God of Jacob", which implies that He loves and redeems the helpless sinner.

In the psalmist's description of God, we can see that Jesus Christ on earth did these very things. He not only gave sight to the physically blinded and healed those who were "bowed down" (Matt. 9:30; Luke 13:30), but He also opened the eyes of the spiritually blinded and raised up those whose spirits were low, as He still does today. God's compassion is the driving force which causes Him to give justice to the oppressed, food to the hungry, relief to the needy and protection to the traveller or the one lonely. Over and over again, we read of the loving-kindnesses of the Lord. This should reinforce to believers who desire to be like Jesus, that we too must show the compassion and love of God.

Prayer for today: *Lord God, thank You for Your inspired Word which is a revelation of Yourself to us. Your greatness is made evident to us in so many ways, and we cannot help but praise You. May we always sense Your presence as You dwell in the midst of our praises.*

Read Psalm 147

Key Verse: Psalm 147:5 *"Great is our Lord, and mighty in power; His understanding is infinite."*

Psalm 147 is truly one of the most pleasant psalms. It has no words of complaint nor any petitions. It is purely a song of praise to the Lord. Because of the references to the building up of Jerusalem (vv. 2, 13-14), it is possible that this psalm was composed after the return from the Exile (as is generally thought of the whole collection of Hallelujah Psalms). They may have been used on the occasion of the dedication of the city wall (Neh. 12:27).

The psalmist encourages the people of the Lord to praise Him, for doing so is good, pleasant, and beautiful. The psalm emphasizes the goodness, omnipotence, and providential care of God for which He deserves to be praised. God has infinite wisdom and under-standing. He not only created all the stars, but He even knows their number and their individual names. Even with our modern technology, scientists have not been able to see all the stars nor can they be numbered. Only the infinite God knows the vastness of the universe. Only He can sustain and care for His creation (vv. 8-9; 16-18). Environmentalists would do well to ask the Lord for His help since He is the One in ultimate control (v. 15). Yet, even though he is the Sovereign Ruler of the universe, He is still concerned about mere man. He heals their broken hearts and binds their wounds. Only the Great Physician can bring healing to the soul and the inner man. Those who have experienced His inner healing have good reason to sing praises and thanksgiving unto the Lord.

The Lord is not impressed with strength, speed, or beauty (v.10), He desires to see humility in the people He has created (v.6). He desires that they love, respect, obey, and reverence Him (all implied in the biblical term "fear"), and also that they put their "hope in His mercy" (v.11). To do this means that they have trusted in Him for His gift of salvation. The greatest mercy of God to mankind was in sending His only begotten Son, our Lord Jesus. Mankind's hope is only found in Him. If we do not believe in Him, we will stand condemned before God. Only through Jesus do we receive atonement for our sins and are made righteous in the sight of God.

The last half of Psalm 147 celebrates God's providential care of His own people who dwell within the city of Jerusalem. It can be understood today as being all those who by faith in Jesus have become citizens of Zion (Eph. 2:19). To them, God gives protection, strength, blessings, and peace.

As the psalmist expressed, God was truly gracious to the ancient Israelites. He chose them to be the recipients of His Holy Word. That was a wonderful privilege. With it came a great responsibility, namely, to be instruments whereby the whole world was to hear of the mercies and judgments of God. Contemplating upon the thought of Israel's election by God, causes the psalmist to close with a loud "hallelujah". We today must be equally enthusiastic with being chosen by God to be His people. Let us also shout hallelujah!

Prayer for today: *Each psalm we read, oh Lord, reminds us of Your majesty and power. We marvel with the psalmist over the fact that though You are the great Creator of our vast universe, You call us Your children and are intimately concerned for us as individuals. We praise You today for Your goodness to us and ask for the wisdom to communicate this truth to others.*

Read Psalms 148, 149&150 June 18

Key Verse: Psalm 150:6 *"Let everything that has breath praise the Lord."*

Psalm 148 calls for the universal praise to the Lord by all created things, both heavenly and earthly, and both living and inanimate. The main reason for His receiving praise is because He is the Creator and the Sustainer. Notice that the crown of God's creation, mankind, is mentioned last for emphasis. Regardless of class, age, or sex, no one is exempt from praising God (148:11-12). Praising God is the main purpose of our being. When people do not praise the Lord and live in obedience to Him, they cannot truly have fulfilled lives. If they think they do, they will discover at the time of the judgment that they were very wrong.

Narrowing it down even further, the psalmist then calls upon God's people to praise Him. They especially have reason to praise God. Only those who have a personal relationship with Jesus Christ can praise God by His Name. They know that His name is Jesus, which is exalted above every other name (148:13; Phil. 2:9-11). A result that comes from praising that name is that God will strengthen and honour those believers and they will be a people who are near to Him, but He also draws nearer to us that we might have a closer fellowship, relationship, and bond.

Psalm 149 gives us yet another dimension of praise. It is the joyful celebration for not only what God has done for us, but for Who God is. We are to rejoice in Him as our Maker and King. For the ancient Israelite, a joyful celebration was accompanied by dancing, singing, and the playing of musical instruments. When the celebration was in honour of the Lord, He would be glorified through this. He would take pleasure in receiving their sincere and joyful praises.

The occasion for this psalm was most likely a military victory for Israel. They received the Lord's help and deliverance and such an important event called for the singing of a "new song"; Thus this psalm was possibly composed for the time when the soldiers returned victoriously from battle. For the believer in Jesus, the new song is the song of salvation and freedom that He puts within our hearts since He has won the victory over sin and death.

Although Israel had won a war, there were still other wars to be waged. They were under the threat of several hostile nations, who were not only their enemies but they were also considered the enemies of God. The sacred Scriptures gave them the authority to destroy them as divine judgment in punishment for their wickedness (149:6-9; Deut. 7:1-2). These verses, however, have been misunderstood in the past by nominal Christians who have used them in support of an actual military assault on the heathen, a holy war. In light of the New Testament, such an interpretation is unacceptable and it ignores the words of the Apostle Paul, "For the weapons of our warfare are not carnal but mighty in God for pulling down [spiritual] strongholds" (2 Cor. 10:4). It is no coincidence that the writer to the Hebrews refers to the double-edged sword as being the Word of God (Heb. 4:12). When believers today praise God it should be accompanied by the sword of the Spirit, not the sword of steel (149:6b; Eph. 6:17). We fight against principalities and powers of darkness over which we will prevail and be victorious by the power of God's Spirit.

What a grand finale is **Psalm 150**! Within the six short verses we read the word "praise" (Hebrew halel) thirteen times! We learn that since God is holy He is to be praised in a holy place — His sanctuary or Temple and in the heavenlies (150:1). We, who make up the Church of Jesus Christ, have been made holy, and our bodies have been made the temple of God so we can be assured that the praises we offer unto Him are acceptable and pleasing (1 Cor. 3:16).

We also learn why we should praise Him. Indeed, we should praise Him for His mighty acts, but primarily we should praise Him for "His excellent greatness." Jesus Christ personified God's greatness, for He was and is the greatest revelation of God to mankind and we today must praise God for Jesus (2 Peter 1:17).

How are we to praise God? With every form of praise, including musical instruments of all kinds, but most importantly we are to praise Him from our own mouths as long as we breathe. He who breathed life into us is worthy of our praise all the days that He has given us upon the earth. Even in eternity, when we have new and resurrected bodies in the life everlasting, we will live to praise Him.

Prayer for today: *Lord God, we live only to praise You and lift up Your name before all people. All our other earthly tasks seem so insignificant compared to being in Your holy presence. Thank You for the access to Your presence You have provided through Jesus. Help us to express to others this treasured access and win them for You.*

Read Titus 1 June 19

Key Verse: 1 Titus 1:16 *"They profess to know God, but in works they deny Him, being abominable, disobedient, and disqualified for every good work."*

As pointed out in the introduction, the Pastoral Epistles were concerned about establishing and defending a sound Christian orthodoxy in the developing churches of Asia Minor. Even as Christianity spread, heresies (or false teachings) were spreading, just like weeds encroaching on a freshly ploughed and planted garden. In this chapter, Paul encourages Titus to "silence" the false teachers (v.11).

A significant factor in the false teaching encroaching upon the Cretan church was the division of creation into spirit and matter — with spirit seen as pure, and matter seen as evil. To these teachers, anything material was evil. Thus they had a low view of creation, everything material being corrupt — that's why Paul refers to them as "those who [themselves] are corrupted" and to whom "nothing is pure" (v.15b). But Paul sets the record straight: "to the pure, all things are pure" (v.15a); that is, purity is a function of mind and conscience. Material things are morally neutral. In other words, there's nothing intrinsically wrong with a match — it's what you do with it. You can start a fire in your fireplace and enjoy its soothing heat, or you can torch an apartment building and destroy human lives. Darkness is the domain of the soul.

This is why Paul says that verbal Christianity is essentially hollow. It's what you do that tells the story of faith or unfaith (v.16). God doesn't need our "vote" (He can, after all, make the trees and rocks cry out His praise). What He does honour is our obedient action as we submit to the law of Christ's love.

Prayer for today: *Father, we long to profess You this day, not only in our words but in our every action. As we look daily into Your Word with open and obedient hearts, bless us with an ever-increasing knowledge of Your absolute goodness and love towards us.*

Read Titus 2 June 20

Key Verse: Titus 2:13 *"looking for the blessed hope and glorious appearing of our great God and Saviour Jesus Christ..."*

The key verse appears in the context of a paragraph which says, "For the grace of God that brings salvation has appeared to all men. It teaches us to say "NO" to ungodliness and worldly passions, and to live self-controlled, upright and godly lives in this present age, while we wait for the blessed hope — the glorious appearing of our great God and Saviour, Jesus Christ, who gave Himself for us to redeem us from all wickedness and to purify for Himself a people that are His very own, eager to do what is good" (vv.11-14 NIV).

There are several key words in the paragraph: words like "grace...salvation...hope...redeem...purify...good." The word "grace" tells us that God has done something for man which is completely unwarranted — He has offered us "salvation" in Christ. This offer first "appeared to all men" when an angelic announcement was sung over the shepherd's fields outside of Bethlehem. It "appeared" again on a wooden cross at Golgotha, and again in a rich man's empty tomb and again on the Mount of olives as the risen Christ ascended before many witnesses to the Father. The whole purpose of this "appearing" was to "redeem" man from sin. Christ came to "buy back" mankind from the "wages of sin" — certain death gave way to certain life for all who put their trust in Him.

Redemption meant the "purifying" of "a people" for Christ's "very own", a people "eager to do what is good".

The "hope", which Paul calls "blessed and glorious" is that there will be one more "appearance": the return of Christ to receive His own and to establish His throne forever. This return is the great hope of the Church, the "Parousia" that has always been the bottom-line motivation for historic Christianity.

Prayer for today: *We thank You, Father, for Your grace which has broken our once hard hearts of pride and has caused them to cry out with thanksgiving and praise. Your grace has truly taught us to say "no" to all ungodliness and empowers us day by day to live upright and godly lives.*

Read Titus 3 *June 21*

Key Verse: Titus 3:14 *"And let our people also learn to maintain good works to meet urgent needs, that they may not be unfruitful."*

The verb "learn" caught my attention as I read the key verse. The Greek word in the text is "manthano", which in this application means "to learn by use and practice, to acquire the habit of, to be accustomed to." What is it Paul wants "our people" to learn? He wants them to learn to "maintain good works". Every activity undertaken for Christ's sake is to be maintained, but this consistency of action is something that doesn't just happen. It has to be learned; it must become a habit.

How is this to be learned? By "use and practice"; that is, it's learned by doing. So much in life is learned this way. There is no question that a lot of "trial and error", wastage of time and energy, can be avoided by training and education. Once the theoretical is past, however the practical becomes the challenge. All of us know a teacher, pastor, or doctor who got straight "A's" in school but can't practise effectively. The "doing" is where the rubber meets the road.

So we learn by doing. We don't voluntarily disqualify ourselves with reasonable excuses — we simply do what needs to be done. If someone has a need, we meet it. If someone needs help, we do our best to assist. We become "doers of the Word, not hearers only" (Jas.1:22).

I like Paul's practical bent here. He says we're to "do good" in terms of providing the "daily necessities" (NIV) of those whose need crosses our path, and we are to see this good work as an outworking of our Christian productivity. We are to bear fruit.

Prayer for today: *Father, help us to be consistent in the practical doing of Your Word, loving not only in word but in deed and truth. "And let us not lose heart in doing good, for in due time we shall reap if we do not grow weary" (Galatians 6:9).*

Read Philemon   June 22

Key Verse: Philemon 6: *"I pray that you may be active in sharing your faith, so that you will have a full understanding of every good thing we have in Christ."*

It is obvious, as Paul writes to his old friend Philemon, that he had a great deal of respect and love for the man. Philemon must have been a special sort of person, a "kindred spirit" with whom Paul felt entirely comfortable. He talks with Philemon as old friends talk: kindly but to the point.

Before he gets to the point, however, Paul prays for Philemon; that prayer is the key verse. What is of great interest in the prayer is the linkage between "sharing your faith", and having "a full understanding of every good thing we have in Christ." It seems that personal evangelism is more than an end in itself — it is also a learning experience for the evangelist.

Perhaps one of the greatest plus factors in personal evangelism is the fielding of questions. Your friend, workmate or relative will throw all kinds of queries in your direction. Some of them will be smoke screens, others will be sincerely asked, but regardless of the motivation, you've got to come up with the answers. Often that will mean saying, "I don't have the answer, but I'll find out." So you're forced to your Bible, to the library, to your pastor and to whatever else may be available in terms of resources. You learn; and learn some more.

I've often said to people, as I reflect on over twenty years pastoring, that the person who learned the most from my preaching was me. Every time I prepare to preach, I learn. As I preach I learn, and as I write this commentary, I learn. The key is to do more than study. Study, of course, is vital, but more vital still is to communicate what you've learned. Once you've done that, you've really learned.

Prayer for today: *Father, Your Word has brought life and peace to our hearts. We desire that others might also share in Your goodness, and we ask for opportunities to effectively share what You have taught us, knowing that as we give it will again be given to us.*

Introduction to
The Book of Proverbs

The Book of Proverbs is the most unique book among the Wisdom Literature and the most practical book of the Bible. It is truly a guide book for living, for it gives wise instructions, admonitions, and reproof concerning all aspects of life. Although it was written centuries ago, it is just as relevant today as it was then, since it deals with human nature, spirituality, relationships, conduct, etc., and as such it is trans-cultural.

The English word "Proverbs" suggest a collection of short sentences that convey moral truths, but the Hebrew name of the book, Michle, has a much fuller meaning, including the idea of comparisons, rules, oracles, or parables. The purpose of the book is to impart wisdom to the reader, which here is understood more in the moral sense than the intellectual. The instruction in wisdom includes understanding, discretion, discernment, discipline, integrity, and righteousness before God. It is wisdom for living a God-centered and God-pleasing life, so that one may truly have life more abundantly, for both wisdom and life come from God. The motto and theme of the book is "the fear of the Lord is the beginning of wisdom" (1:7; 9:10). The basis of our conduct is found on our knowledge and reverence of God.

The principle author is Solomon, but the last two chapters are ascribed to Agur (chapter 30) and King Lemuel (chapter 31). All we know of them is what we have written in the text, yet it is certain that they were righteous, God-fearing men. There is another portion called "the words of the wise" (22:17-24:34), which may be a compilation of the wise sayings of ancient sages, but it has been argued that this portion was also penned by Solomon, who was by far the wisest of all sages.

The scribes of King Hezekiah, a godly descendant of Solomon who instigated reforms (2 Chron.29:1-3), selected and copied the proverbs of Solomon in chapters 25-29. The historical records show that Solomon composed 3000 proverbs (1 Kings 4:32), and so those found within this book (a total of about 800) would have been selected from a greater body of material.

Solomon loved and feared the Lord. When God asked him what he desired, he answered "wisdom", for he knew how precious and valuable it was (1 Kings3:3, 9-12). Solomon's wisdom was a divine gift. It superceded the wisdom of all the world. He not only

Continued on next page

had spiritual wisdom, but he also had knowledge and understanding of nature (1 Kings 4:29-34; 10:6-9, 23-24).

Among the Hebrews, the men of wisdom were equal to the prophets and priests in their spiritual leadership and in their receiving of divine revelations (cf. Jer. 18:18; Ezek. 7:26). They held prominent places in government and counselled the king. The nation was particularily blessed when the king was also among the wise men.

The Wisdom Literature of Proverbs is in the form of Hebrew poetry which makes use of much figurative language and parallelisms. In it are many comparisons and contrasts that are pointed and direct, having a clear message that tells the sinner to turn from his wicked ways, which lead to destruction, and turn to wisdom, which leads to life. It encourages diligence, truthfulness, and righteousness which spring from wisdom. Our Lord Jesus must have loved the book of Proverbs, since His teaching often echoed it (e.g. compare Prov. 25:6-7 with Luke 14:7-11). In Proverbs, wisdom is often spoken of as though it were a person (e.g. chapter 8), and from the New Testament we learn that the person Jesus is the Wisdom of God and through Him we receive everlasting life (1 Cor. 1:24, 30; Col. 2:2-3).

Special Note: Be sure to write in your request today for your next volume of *DAY UNTO DAY, the Year Two — Summer* edition. It starts July 1!

Read Proverbs 1 June 23

Key Verse: Proverbs 1:7 *"The fear of the Lord is the beginning of knowledge..."*

From the beginning of the Book, we read of the author's intention to give "instruction of wisdom", and who better to teach it than Solomon, the wisest man who ever lived. This first section of the book is specifically addressed to "the young man", yet even one who is older and wiser could benefit from following Solomon's wise counsel (v. 5). He gives practical advice to all who read with open minds and hearts. Before Solomon deals with moral issues, he gives the motto for all the proverbs: "The fear of the Lord is the beginning of knowledge" (v. 7). The first principle for learning knowledge that is of any significance is to believe in God, respect Him, and stand in awe of Him. Also, this important verse is understood as teaching that the first step to a person's morality is his relationship with God.

When a young person fears the Lord, he will also be obedient to his parents. The instruction of both the father and mother in the area of spiritual things is very important for a child's spiritual well-being. The teaching is not meant to be a burden, but rather a pleasant thing that will cause the young person to be honoured and respected, as well as giving him inner beauty and life to his soul (vv. 8-9; 3:22).

The "fool" stands in sharp contrast to the one who fears the Lord. The "fool" does not fear God. He is a sinner who lives his life as though God did not exist, and he is one who does not heed advice; as such, they are the most unwise people (v. 7b). The author warns his student not to be like them nor fall into their temptations: "If sinners entice you, do not consent" (v. 10); their ways lead to self-destruction. They are self-willed and greedy and enjoy doing evil. They prey on innocent victims to become rich by dishonest gain. These professional thieves are more stupid than birds, for even birds at least have the sense to stay far from a net that is set in their view. The fools, however, set the net to catch others, and although they are aware of the trap, they themselves fall prey to it and die (vv. 11-19).

Solomon's plea for his student to attain wisdom continues by illustrating his lesson with the person of wisdom, who in this section appears as a woman. Wisdom calls out to three types of people: the simple who are naive and can easily be swayed to sin; the scorners who mock at the righteous and take pleasure in evil; and the most wicked of people, the fools who hate the truth or anything having to do with God. Even these people can be turned from their path of destruction. If they would only turn away from sin and seek the truth, then wisdom would gladly and graciously pour her spirit upon them. If they stubbornly refuse the mercy she extends to them and do not heed her calling unto them, then the period of grace will be over (v. 28); it will be too late for them, since they did not choose to fear the Lord, and their own self-reliance and life without God will lead them to destruction (cf. Romans 1:18-32). Wisdom promises, however, that those who do turn to her will dwell safely and securely, without having to fear evil. Our Lord Jesus was the true personification of divine wisdom (Col. 2:3; 1 Cor. 1:24, 30), and all who turn to Him will dwell safely in everlasting life with Him, where there will be no presence of evil.

Prayer for today: Oh Lord, like Solomon, we ask for Your divine wisdom to be given to us liberally, for it is only through such wisdom that we can handle life's circumstances and help others through godly counsel.

Read Proverbs 2 &3

Key Verse: Proverbs 3:5-6 "Trust in the Lord with all your heart, and lean not on your own understanding; in all your ways acknowledge Him, and He shall direct your paths."

Solomon begins the second lesson in chapter 2 by telling his student of the benefits that follow a diligent search for wisdom. If, with his whole heart, he earnestly seeks wisdom (which includes discernment and understanding), zealously seeking as though it were hidden treasure, then he would learn that it only comes from God. His search would lead him to understand the fear of God, and thus come to know God personally. We too must make it our goal to attain wisdom by going to the Lord who is glad to give wisdom to those who seek Him and ask for it (James 1:5). He will protect, guard, and preserve His children to whom He has given wisdom, as they walk the path of righteousness.

When wisdom is treasured in one's heart, it results in spiritual strength. The believer is given discretion and understanding, which will serve to deliver him from evil. He will be able to discern the tricks of the enemy and know when there is a distortion of truth; thus he will be preserved from such evils that are practiced by the perverse man and the seductive adulteress. A life of immorality is very dangerous — "for the wages of sin is death" (Rom. 6:23). This same verse in the Book of Romans ends on the same note as does this chapter of Proverbs: "but the gift of God is eternal life through Christ Jesus our Lord." Those who are upright and keep to the paths of righteousness will "dwell in the land" and "remain in it" (2:21). This refers to their inheritance within the Promised Land, but it ultimately means that the pure in heart will dwell in the glorious eternal inheritance of heaven, whereas the wicked will have no part in it (3:35).

In Proverbs 3, Solomon asks his student to keep his commands in his heart. His commands are actually the commands of God which Solomon has claimed as his own and is teaching. Note the blessing which results from keeping the Word of God: a long and peaceful life (3:2; Deut. 8:1). As Solomon stresses, God's word (His mercy and truth) is to be kept in the believer's heart (3:1, 3). We are not merely to perform outward acts of obedience and have only a head knowledge of the Word of God; it must come from within our hearts. When God's Word is an integral part within us, then we will not sin against Him, and we will find favour and honour in the sight of God and man (3:4).

The famous verse, "trust in the Lord with all your heart", assures believers that if they trust God wholeheartedly rather than relying on their own intellect and finite wisdom, they will be blessed with God's guidance. If we truly fear God, we will recognize Him in all we do, and then He will keep us on the right track (3:5-6). He will also bless us with health, prosperity, and life. Fearing God means that we obey Him and do all we can to please and honour Him. As Solomon instructed, one way to honour God is to give Him our tithes and offerings, which really belong to God anyway, like the first-fruits (Ex. 22:29; Deut. 18:4). If we do so, He promises to bless us with prosperity (Deut. 28:2, 8), which in the New Testament period means primarily the prosperity of the soul, as it is far more important than material wealth.

Even chastisement is a blessing from the Lord. Since He loves His people, He corrects them as a good and loving Father would correct his child. The purpose of some afflictions is that God's children might not follow the wrong path that leads to death but that, in turning to God, they might find wisdom and treasure her above any other thing. Because they trust in God, they will not be caught in the net of the wicked, nor do they need to fear or worry about anything (3:25-26). This is the truly blessed kind of life that is available to all people. Pray that others will listen and turn to the voice of wisdom that is calling out to them and know this voice is the voice of Jesus our Lord (cf. 1:20-23).

Prayer for today: *Gracious Lord, we acknowledge You in every area of our lives, because without You we are nothing. Thank You for Your wonderful promise to guide us as we keep You at the very top of our priorities. And though Your ways may conflict with our limited understanding, still we will trust You.*

Read Proverbs 4&5 *June 25*

Key Verse: Proverbs 4:23 *"Keep your heart with all diligence, for out of it spring the issues of life."*

As we are told from the beginning of Proverbs 4, Solomon was fortunate to have a father that impressed upon him the importance and necessity of attaining wisdom and serving God with a loyal heart (1 Chron. 28:9). King David's words were indeed retained in Solomon's heart (4:4), for when God asked Solomon what he wanted, he remembered the words of his father and, as is well known, his response was "give me wisdom and knowledge" (2 Chron. 1:10; cf. 1 Kings 3:5-9). The Lord happily granted Solomon's request, which is not only attested to in history (1 Kings 4:29-30; 2 Chron. 9:5-6) but is evidenced in this Book of Proverbs. His father David had told him that if he embraced and exalted wisdom as he would a most beloved wife, then wisdom would promote him and bring him honour. David illustrated this by referring to the ancient practice in the marriage ceremony when the bride would put a wreath ("a crown of glory") upon the bridegroom's head (4:9).

Like his father, Solomon instructed his children in the way of wisdom, but it appears he was especially attentive to the son who would succeed him upon the throne (compare 4:1 "my children" to 4:10, 20, "my son"). The spiritual and political welfare of the nation was often dependent upon the type of king that ruled over them. The history of Israel attests to the fact that when godly kings reigned, having the wisdom of God to guide them, it went well with the nation.

The wise advice to the student (who is a person of any age) is to take hold of wise instruction and not let it go, for it will bring life. The path of the wicked, however, is a path of darkness which is to be avoided and shunned at all costs. In total contrast, the path of the righteous is like a bright light and those who faithfully continue to travel upon it all the days of their life get ever closer to the source of that light and closer to the "perfect day" when they will stand before the Lord Jesus, the Light of the World (4:18; John 1:9).

In our walk of faith, we must be careful to diligently guard our hearts from any impurity, as well as carefully consider the path we are taking and resolve to keep our eyes on the Lord, for if we do that we will not stray from the right path (4:23, 25-26). If one's mouth speaks lies and perversity, then it shows that the heart within is equally perverse (4:24; Matt. 15:18-19). But if we feed on the Word of God and upon pure and lovely things, then equally lovely things will come out of our mouths and bring forth life as well as health in all areas: mind, body and soul (4:21-22), which all spring from the peace of God in our hearts (Phil. 4:8-9; Luke 6:45).

An important part of the life-giving divine wisdom taught by Solomon in chapter 5 is marital fidelity, as he gives a strong warning to stay far from, and not even consider, sexual immorality. Solomon begins by warning his student about the evils of adultery. The immoral person's lips are full of flattery and sweet sounding words of enticement, but in actuality, what appears to be honey turns out to be the most bitter of all herbs; what was thought to be satisfying and soothing (like oil) turns out to be a sharp sword that breaks a person a part, gives a fatal blow, and cuts him off from the blessings of God (4:4; 10-11). As Solomon continues, he appears to speak from personal experience, saying that those who commit adultery will be the losers and will certainly come to regret it, for it will put them to public shame and leave them on the verge of total ruin (4:12-14) unless they repent and the Lord intervenes to forgive and restore wisdom.

With an illustration of a fountain of water, Solomon shows the importance and rightness of remaining faithful to one's spouse, for only with that person will there ever be true and lasting satisfaction, and God will bless them because of their fidelity in honouring their marriage covenant (5:18). God sees all that mankind does, even in the privacy of the bedroom, so Solomon warns that the one who persistently lives promiscuously will be known by God and receive the punishment due him. His sinful foolishness in leaving God and His ways will entrap him and he will have reached the point where he can no longer receive instruction or God's grace; thus he will die in sin (cf. Rom. 1:28-32).

Prayer for today: *Dear Lord, we pray that You would reveal to us the importance of that which we put into our hearts, for it affects all aspects of our lives. May we fill our hearts so full of You and Your Word that there would be no room for negative influences.*

Key Verse: Proverbs 6:23 *"For the commandment is a lamp, and the law is light; reproofs of instruction are the way of life."*

Solomon continues to give instruction and advice about being wise in commercial dealings. He warns his student against rashly pledging himself as surety, so that his friend might be given a loan. The motivation behind becoming the guarantor was likely pride in himself, his achievements, and money, and it displayed a trust in others that could prove disastrous. We can only be one hundred percent sure of our trust in God but not in our fellow man. There must have been corrupt business practices during the time of Solomon, and he did not want to see his student fall into the trap and loose everything, as he may have seen happen to others. Solomon warns the student that if he ever unthinkingly and unwisely did such a thing, he should immediately realize his grave mistake, humble himself, swallow his pride, and persistently plead to be relieved of his obligation before it is too late (vv. 1-5).

Solomon encourages industry and hard work, which is the way to prevent poverty. He mocks at the "sluggard", for an ant is wiser than such a person. From the other uses of the word "sluggard" or "slothful" within the book of Proverbs, we come to understand that the word implies not just a lazy person but one who is also a fool or a sinner (compare 15:19; 21:25-26; 26:13-16). He can learn much from the ant by watching its discipline, diligence, perseverance, co-operation, and even prudence. When a person is idle, he leaves himself more open to temptation and sin, such as happened to David when he sinned with Bathsheba (2 Sam. 11:1-4).

The next type of person that Solomon describes is one who is not slothful but even more worthless. He busies himself with stirring up dissension and deception, and he is always devising evil. Everything he does outwardly, with his mouth, eyes, feet, and fingers (possibly referring rude gestures) reflect the perversity of his heart (v. 12-14). Just as he sows discord, so will he reap the calamity upon himself that discord brings. God hates his sinful ways and Solomon lists them in the form of a numerical proverb. The six that are listed are a background for the seventh, upon which lies the emphasis. The same thought was introduced before: "He sows discord" (v. 14), and now Solomon lists that particular evil as the worst: "discord among brethren". The Lord, however, is most pleased with a peacemaker and loves to see people dwelling together in unity (cf. Matt. 5:9; Ps. 133:1; Col. 3:15).

The one who fears the Lord, obeys His commandments, and heeds the instructions of his parents will be blessed and will also be a blessing to others. Moses had instructed the people to put the Law of God upon them and within their hearts as a constant reminder of their obligation to obedience. Solomon reaffirms this same practice by instructing his son to do likewise with his godly and wise teachings (v. 21; Deut. 6:6-9). If a person treasures the Word of God in his heart, then it will always serve as a lamp to lead, keep, and even speak to him. The Word, however, may speak words of reproof, which serve to convict of sin, and thus preserve one from falling into sin and keep him headed on "the way of life" (v. 23). The wisdom from God's Word will tell him to stay far from the harlot or anyone who continually practices sin, for that is the way of destruction, poverty, and ultimately death (v. 26).

Prayer for today: *We praise You today, dear God, for Your Word. May we not be slothful in our Christian walk but wholly trust and obey Your Word, as it sheds Light on our path and convicts us of sin.*

Read Proverbs 7&8   *June 27*

Key Verse: Proverbs 8:11 *"For wisdom is better than rubies, and all the things one may desire cannot be compared with her."*

Once again, Solomon stresses the importance of his student heeding his instructions, so that he may realize the dangers of adultery and fornication and thus stay far away from the seductress, that he may have life and not death. It is just as important today that the Lord's Word be treasured and guarded within our hearts as one would guard the most precious and important part of the eye — the pupil. That is the part of the eye that lets in the light, and if it is harmed, the person will live in darkness. Solomon wants his student to feel insepa-rable with wisdom and understanding, as though they were his nearest relatives with whom he had a close and personal relationship and upon whom he could depend for help in time of need (7:4).

With graphic details, Solomon tells the dramatic story of the young man who, lacking understanding, fell prey to the loud and rebellious woman who seduced him. He was foolish to be out wan-dering the streets at night and passing by "her corner". A servant of the Lord must keep far from any appearance of evil and must keep busy in the work of the Lord so that he might not have the idle time to get lured into sinful snares. The evil woman caught the young man in her trap when he got too close. He was quick to yield to the temptation. His sin, a temporal pleasure, would bring severe and lasting consequences, namely death (James 1:14-16). Truly he followed her like an ox to the slaughter (7:22)

The depth of sin and hypocrisy in the wicked woman is revealed by her invitation for him to come into her home on a religious pretext: to eat of the peace offering with her, since her husband was away and she was ceremonially clean. She used this as an opportunity to fulfill her lustful desires (cf. Lev. 7:11, 19-20). She may have been ceremonially clean, but inwardly she was filthy and defiled, and she brought defilement upon the young man as well. Although only a woman, she had caused the destruction of many strong and great men (7:26). This strong warning that Solomon gave centuries ago is just as relevant today. It teaches us that no matter how great or small we think we are, we all need the wisdom and understanding of God to withstand temptation. "Therefore let him who thinks he stands take heed lest he fall" (1 Cor. 10:12).

Chapter eight is a poem wherein wisdom is again personified. To properly understand this chapter, we must see Jesus Christ as the wisdom who speaks out to the people. Jesus referred to Himself, as did the Apostle Paul, as "the wisdom of God" (Luke 11:49; 1 Cor. 1:24). The wonderful attributes of wisdom as seen here are those of Jesus the Messiah (Isa. 11:2). We also learn here of wisdom's role in creation, and we know that Jesus Christ was with God in creation. He was that wisdom that was with God from the beginning and that was established from everlasting (8:22-23; Col. 1:15-18; John 1-3).

Unlike the seductive voice in the darkness, wisdom's voice speaks out in the daylight at public places to all who would listen, for the Lord does not want any to perish (2 Pet. 3:9). He wants people to diligently seek Him, ask for wisdom, and receive it (James 1:5; Luke 11:9-13). Wisdom speaks true, pure, and excellent things that can be understood by all those who love her (Matt. 13:16, 23). Nothing immoral, deceptive, or perverse can come from her mouth, for such wickedness is an abomination to her. Wisdom admonishes all people to receive her and desire her over and above material possessions, for nothing can compare with her (8:11). No amount of wealth can save a person, but wisdom can deliver a person from destruction.

The same attributes and blessings of wisdom are paralleled in Jesus and His relationship with us. He truly gives wonderful and generous rewards to those who have Him in their hearts. He gives honour and "enduring [spiritual] riches and righteousness" (8:18). He causes those who seek and love Him to inherit wealth: the meek and the righteous shall inherit the earth and "theirs is the kingdom of God" (Matt. 5:5, 10). He fills their treasuries, giving their longing souls satisfaction (8:21). Wisdom's words are those of Jesus, "For whoever finds me finds life, and obtains favor from the Lord", but those who reject and despise the "Wisdom of God" will destroy themselves (8:36; 1 John 5:12; 1 Cor. 1:24).

We, as Christian, should long to have our hearts filled with Jesus and the divine wisdom, understanding, knowledge, discernment, and integrity that is available to us who love and seek Him, that we may bear the good fruits of wisdom (8:19; see Eph. 1:17; Col. 1:9-10; James 3:17).

Prayer for today: *Dear Father, You have revealed true and perfect wisdom in the person of Your Son, our Lord and Saviour Jesus Christ. May we desire Him more than anything else, for material possessions are so temporary, but our relationship with Jesus is eternal.*

Read Proverbs 9&10   June 28

Key Verse: Proverbs 10:16 *"The labor of the righteous leads to life, the wages of the wicked to sin."*

Wisdom graciously sends out her invitation to the simple, asking him to come and feast in her house that is held up by seven pillars. The number seven is symbolic of complete perfection and holiness. She extends her invitation to the simple: those who are naive and can easily be enticed to sin; these are the ones most susceptible to respond positively to her invitation. The foolish woman's target is this same type of person (9:16), but what a contrast there is between the results of wisdom's banquet and the fool's!

Those who agree to enter into wisdom's banquet first receive nourishment, are filled and satisfied. When we come to Jesus, that is the first thing He does for us; then afterwards we live with Him in His holy household made up of the body of believers; we are able to listen to His words of wisdom and instruction from His Holy Word and upon this we continue to feed daily (John 6:35). In wisdom's house, one finds joy, life, and understanding. In sharp contrast, the dark banquet of the wicked woman is attended by the dead in the depths of hell.

When those who abide with the Lord try to reprove and change the behaviour of a scoffer (a foolish person who does not fear God, but openly acts in disobedience and defiance of God), they end up being scorned; they have no effect, because the scoffer will not listen to them. The Lord can and has saved this type of person, but only once he has come to Jesus and have received knowledge of Him, "the Holy One", thereby attaining understanding (9:10); only then can a fellow believer reprove him with love, and with the conviction of the Holy Spirit, he will change his ways to become more like Christ.

The second section of the Book of Proverbs begins with chapter ten and continues through 22:16. In this section, entitled "The Proverbs of Solomon", there are 375 different proverbs that have been inspired by Wisdom. Interestingly, in the Hebrew language, letters are also used in numbering, and the sum of the letters in the name of Solomon add up to 375. The compiler likely selected these particular proverbs of Solomon purposefully from a larger collection (cf. 1 Kings 4:32), and, to honour Solomon and attest to his authorship, selected 375. Many of them are related, covering a wide range of topics that deal with practical wisdom. Most of them take the form of contrasts.

In chapter ten, the dominant topic appears to be the contrast between the godly, industrious, and diligent man of understanding who is successful and prosperous, as opposite to the wicked, lazy man who is poor, sinful, and in adversity. The righteous and wise son makes his father glad, but in contrast the sinful ("foolish") and lazy son brings shame to his parents, and particularly grief to his mother (10:1, 5).

Their respective rewards are likewise opposite. The wise man receives a long list of blessings: riches, honour (even after his death, 10:7), security, fulfilment, an everlasting foundation upon the Solid Rock, prolonged days, hope, gladness, strength, and the greatest reward: life everlasting, for he will never be removed from his eternal inheritance in God's kingdom (10:16-17, 30; cf. Matt. 5:5, 10; John 3:16). The wicked man, on the other hand, has no part in God's kingdom; he will fall, be impoverished and have a bad reputation; his expectations will perish and he will see destruction and death.

Yet another contrast is shown with regard to the love of the righteous (the wise) and the hate of the wicked (the fool), which is evident in the words of their mouth, as well as their actions. "Hatred stirs up strife", which is the desire of the wicked (cf. 6:14, 19). They speak perverse words, full of lying and slander, which cause violence and discord. What will this bring upon themselves? Their tongue will be cut out and they will be destroyed. The love of the righteous, however, "covers all sins" (10:12; 1 Pet. 4:8; James 5:20; 1 Cor. 13:4-8). Their words are like a "well of life" (10:11). They revive and renew the strength of others. They bring healing, growth, edification, and encouragement. They are words of wisdom, which are fitly chosen like "choice silver" (10:20), unlike the fool who speaks whatever comes into his perverse mind (cf. Eph. 4:29; 5:4; James 3:1-12). Let us, like the psalmist, ask for God's help, strength, and wisdom: "Set a guard, O Lord, over my mouth; keep watch over the door of my lips" (Ps. 141:3).

Prayer for today: What great blessings You give, oh God, to the righteous who live in Your wisdom! Put a watch over our mouths this day, that we might speak only that which will bring encouragement, healing, and growth to others.

Read Proverbs 11 June 29

Key Verse: Proverbs 11:30 *"The fruit of the righteous is a tree of life, and he who wins souls is wise."*

Solomon's proverbs continue with stressing the importance of honesty in business dealings, for that pleases the Lord. "A false balance" is a way to cheat others, springing out of greed and a disregard for one's neighbours — this is an abomination to the Lord (11:1; Lev. 19:35-36). The root cause is pride and a selfish desire to be great and rich, which the fool will try to attain by any means, even though it harms his neighbour. He is ruthless and unprincipled. He will withhold grain to cause the prices to rise, but this will cause the poor to curse him (11:26). Such perversity and pride will bring him shame and cause his fall (11:2; 16:18), as well as the destruction of all his hopes and expectations. The riches he lusted after and attained through corrupt means will profit him nothing on judgment day, when God's wrath will be poured out upon him.

The presence of too many wicked men, such as the one described above, will bring the downfall of their city and break apart the society. The opposite is true if there are enough righteous men within the city (e.g. Sodom and Gomorrah, Gen. 18:32); their wise counsel to the leader will bring safety (11:14; 24:6; compare 1 Kings 12:1-14, where foolish counsel brought about the division of the kingdom). Wise men deal honestly and prudently and cause the city to rejoice and be exalted (11:10-11). The people will bless the man who sells his grain at an honest price (11:26). He will be successful, since wisdom and integrity will guide him, and his righteousness will deliver him from death (11:4).

Unlike the foolish, the wise work to maintain peace; they do not gossip or reveal secrets which can stir up trouble and bring hurt to a person, but instead they use discretion. They can be trusted as faithful confidantes to "conceal a matter" (11:12-13; 19:11). Such a person is merciful and full of grace and therefore retains his honour, as does the "gracious woman". The one, however, who is cruel and ruthless may retain riches but will never retain honour, and he is destined to fall (11:16, 28). The righteous please God and "flourish like foliage" (11:28). They receive honour and divine favour because of their blameless ways, which are far more important than riches (11:16, 27). Even so, the righteous will be judged and suffer the recompense because of their sinful nature, but how much more will the wicked sinner be recompensed with divine wrath (11:31; 1 Pet. 4:17-19).

The wisdom and understanding of the righteous yields fruit, for they are like a tree of life (Ps. 1:3). By their witness for God and their example to others, who see them flourish and have true life, they bring other souls to share in this tree of life that only God can give. The truly wise are those who purpose in their heart to win souls, for that is what the Lord desires His people to do (be "fishers of men", Matt. 4:19; Eph. 5:15-17). Their divinely given wisdom teaches them their responsibility to win souls. Also, wisdom, coupled with love, instructs them in the best way to bring others to the Lord, that they too may know and experience the Lord and the wisdom He gives (James 5:20; Ezek. 3:17-21; Dan. 12:3).

Prayer for today: *You, oh God, are the Author of Wisdom, and You write it in our hearts by Your Holy Spirit. Make us fruitful trees of life You can use to attract and win souls for Your eternal Kingdom.*

Read Proverbs 12   June 30

Key Verse: Proverbs 12:28 *"In the way of righteousness is life, and in its pathway there is no death."*

Proverbs 12 deals with contrasts in conduct between several opposing pairs: the righteous man and the wicked man, the virtuous woman and the one who brings shame to her husband, the industrious man and the slothful man, the wise man and the foolish man. The one who loves and heeds the counsel and reproof of wisdom is wise. He is one who loves knowledge and is described as a good man who obtains favour from the Lord (12:1-2). Those who hate reproof are stupid; they are the fools who think going their own way is right and disregard the way of the Lord. Fools live out their days without having understanding or without growing as a person. Rather than using their minds and wills with integrity, they use their resources to devise wickedness,and are thus despised and condemned by God.

The excellent wife brings honour to her husband. The term translated as "excellent" has a fuller meaning; it literally means "a woman of valour". In other places, the word is used to describe a good soldier. To hold the fort or maintain the order and peace of the household takes many excellent qualities which are described further in 31:10-31. Among them are wisdom, strength, and virtue, which serve her well in being a godly influence in her home and in fulfilling her domestic duties. However, the foolish wife, who brings shame to her husband, is like "rottenness in his bones", which continues to rot like a cancer until he collapses. Her entire household will collapse, but "the house of the righteous will stand" (12:7). When the people of God are firmly rooted in Him and established in His Word, they may sway a little during the storms of life, but nothing can uproot them. The wicked, however, are blown away like chaff in the wind (12:3).

The righteous are kindhearted, not only to man but also to their animals, which they treat with concern for their well-being (cf. Deut. 25:4). They know that God is the Creator of all things, and therefore they, like the Lord, show tender mercies to animals and show even more love to their fellow man (Matt. 6:26). The wicked, however, who do not fear God, have no regard or respect for any of God's creatures, be it man or animal. They are so depraved that what they think to be tender mercies to their animals are in fact cruelties (12:10).

Yet another contrast in conduct is drawn between the wise, hard worker and the foolish, lazy man. The wise man may have to do some menial tasks himself and thereby be lightly esteemed, yet he still has managed his finances well enough to have at least one servant, and since he works the land, he will have sufficient food to eat. On the other hand, the fool who is too proud and lazy to do lowly jobs would rather go hungry. He is "devoid of understanding" , for he does not work hard but "follows frivolity", such as dreaming up get-rich-quick schemes and hoping to get lucky by finding buried treasure or, in today's terms, by winning the lottery. The fool's hopes, however, will perish (12:7). He will end up being the servant to the one who works diligently (12:24).

A final dominant contrast is shown between the truthful dealings of the righteous man and the deceitful and lies of the wicked. The wicked will be ensnared by his lies, but because of the truth that the righteous man speaks, he will come through trouble and the Lord will delight in Him. His words bring health and satisfaction, and he will have peace and joy and be established forever, unlike the man with the lying tongue, whose words are like a sword and who will be gone like a vapour (12:17-22). Considering the contrasts, one does wisely to follow Solomon's advice and choose his friends carefully, since they can have either a good or an adverse influence. Let us be careful to not be pulled down or led astray by the wicked. Let us rather be filled with wisdom, that we might be stronger and have a positive influence on others, directing them toward the way of righteousness through Jesus.

Prayer for today: *We praise You today, oh Lord, for the practical wisdom You have revealed to us in Your Word. Who better than You, our Creator, knows how we should live in order to have a fulfilling and abundant life? We re-commit ourselves today to follow Your Word more fully.*

Proclaiming the Good News of Jesus
— Since 1962 —

THE CROSSROADS CHRISTIAN COMMUNICATIONS FAMILY OF MINISTRIES:

100 HUNTLEY STREET: Daily Christian television since 1977. Viewers obtain counselling and prayer through dozens of telephone counselling centres.

CIRCLE SQUARE: Top quality Christian programming for children. This fast-paced weekly show is popular in many countries around the world.

CIRCLE SQUARE RANCHES: Started as a follow-up to the Circle Square program, there are now nine ranches offering summer camping programs for children and year-round retreats.

CMP: Christian Missions Productions has produced Christian programs in 17 languages other than English.

NITE LITE: Late night live open-line television in which the host matches real problems of callers with the answers of the Gospel.

HEART TO HEART FAMILY MINISTRIES: Marriage and family counselling and seminars promoting Biblical wholeness in the home.

KINGDOM ADVENTURE: State-of-the-art children's programming combining puppetry and animation to teach Biblical truths and values.

CHRISTIAN BROADCAST ACADEMY: Television production training for men and women of vision who want this medium used for the Gospel.

DAVID MAINSE CRUSADES: Interdenominational, area-wide evangelistic crusades.

E.R.D.F.: The Emergency Response and Development Fund: For years, TV viewers have responded whenever stories of human need have been featured.

If you would like information on becoming a partner with us through your prayerful and financial support, please write your request to: C.C.C.I., 100 Huntley Street, Toronto, Ontario, Canada M4Y 2L1.

Notes

Notes

Notes

Notes

Notes